PRAISE FOR *ONE SHOT...*

One Shot is a great book to help men understand the life God destined us to live. We were made for Him. We were made for each other.

—*Raymond Berry,*
NFL Hall of Fame player for the Baltimore Colts and
former head coach of the New England Patriots

Thought provoking, insightful and biblical, *One Shot* illuminates what a life of faith is all about.

—*Mike Coleman,*
cofounder and CEO of Integrity Music

How do you sum up the message of *One Shot*? Surrender and bravery. Two words you don't often see together. Surrender is all about releasing control of your self-centered life and turning it over to Christ. Bravery comes when you take up the challenge to risk it all for the cause of Christ. I highly recommend *One Shot.*

—*Todd Chobotar,*
Director of Publishing at Florida Hospital,
America's largest hospital

When Jesus said *"Come, follow Me,"* He called us to a life of adventure in Him, a life of love and sacrifice of heroic proportions....This book is a catalyst for that adventure. Todd has given us the encouragement to step out, look into the future, and follow God with all of our heart!

—*Dr. Ed Litton,*
senior pastor and filmmaker

Todd Burkhalter challenges us all to take the risk and examine our belief system with potential change toward deeper relationships. He explains how the adventure on the road less traveled leads to true significance. This is a must-read for all men today!

—*Bill Irwin,*
author of Blind Courage *and the only blind man to hike the 2,168-mile Appalachian Trail—alone (www.billirwin.com)*

Todd Burkhalter gets us beyond the surface—beyond what can be seen—so we can focus on what really matters in life and adjust our courses accordingly.

—*Bob Cornuke,*
former police investigator, SWAT team member, biblical investigator, international explorer, and best-selling author

Goes where few books are willing to go. A great spiritual foundation for a dynamic life that brings glory to God.

—*Chris Thomason,*
president of Indelible Media

I've spent my life working with men and women who risk their lives for others. *One Shot* calls us to respond. We waste our lives if we aren't living for something we would die for. I can't recommend this book highly enough.

—*W. Michael Moore,*
captain, US Coast Guard

We are called to a life of purpose and passion. Todd has done a great job of writing about a life of significance—a life lived for eternity. Start your adventure for truth today with *One Shot.*

—*Dr. Dow Robinson,*
Wycliffe Bible Translator, translated the New Testament into Aztec and lived twenty-five years among Aztecs of Mexico

ONESHOT

LIVING A LIFE OF FAITH AT FULL SPEED

ONESHOT

LIVING A LIFE OF FAITH AT FULL SPEED

TODD BURKHALTER

WITH TODD HILLARD

WHITAKER
HOUSE

MID-CONTINENT PUBLIC LIBRARY - BTM

3 0003 00807820 4

ONE SHOT:
Living a Life of Faith at Full Speed

ISBN-13: 978-1-60374-071-5
ISBN-10: 1-60374-071-6
Printed in the United States of America
© 2007, 2008 by Todd Burkhalter

Whitaker House
1030 Hunt Valley Circle
New Kensington, PA 15068
www.whitakerhouse.com

Library of Congress Cataloging-in-Publication Data

Burkhalter, Todd, 1963–
One shot : living a life of faith at full speed / by Todd Burkhalter ;
with Todd Hillard.
p. cm.
Summary: "Encourages men to trust the Bible and live a life of adventure, challenge, and significance based on its principles"—Provided by publisher.
ISBN 978-1-60374-071-5 (trade pbk. : alk. paper) 1. Men—Religious life.
I. Hillard, Todd, 1963– II. Title.
BV4528.2.B88 2008
248.8'42—dc22
                              2008020237

1 2 3 4 5 6 7 8 9 10 11 **ய** 15 14 13 12 11 10 09 08

DEDICATION

To my boys, Jackson, Christian, and Bishop; and our baby girl, Holland…

who will one day read this book and who, I pray, will have seen it lived out in their father.

And to my mom, Annie…

God's love makes perfect sense to me because I saw it in you. I miss you.

ACKNOWLEDGMENTS

Jenny, my beloved… *You are above all others.*

Quinton James Jackson, Christian William Andrew, Bishop Frederick Todd, Holland Anne, my little lambs… *I love you guys. I'm so proud to be known as your father. It's my favorite title. "For the glory of God and no other," go full speed.*

Wayne Burkhalter, my dad… *Pop, we're best friends. Thanks for helping me believe.*

Nancy and Allen James, our parents… *Thank you for your insight and prayers as we literally worked side by side. I love you.*

Todd Hillard… *I have learned so much through writing a book with you. Thank you for your optimism and faith.*

Todd Chobotar… *This book would not be possible without your friendship, creativity, wisdom, and generosity.*

The PK Team: Brad Nixon, Mark Walker, Chantell Hinkle, Gordon England, and Jeff Rasor… *You are soldiers, fighting a very real war. Thank you for your prayers and support. Your spiritual oversight in the content and editing of this book has been invaluable.*

Harold Velasquez… *The PK relationship, and effectively this book, started with my great love and respect for you.*

Mike Coleman... *Mentor, friend, and partner in a vision. Thank you for everything.*

Brent Reese, Alan Phillips, and Chris Strickland, my oldest friends... *We came to Christ together and by God's grace we continue together in faith. Love you guys.*

Mark Berry, Roger Severino, David Cropp, Kenny Pegram, and Chris Thomason... *To a lifelong band of brothers who challenge me and remind me of where my significance lies.*

Our small group and friends: Jim and Sonya Wentland, Doug and Bette Meduna, Kevin and Aimee Wiemer, Shane and LaJuan Black, Mike and Amy Reed, and Mike and Renee Moore... *You continue to shape our understanding of the active expression of the love of God.*

Pastor Jim Bryars and Grace Community Church... *My humble thanks to you and our church family for your generosity and support during the research and writing of the manuscript. "How great the Father's love for us, How great beyond all measure."*

Ed Litton... *Thank you for your wisdom and good counsel at the start of this book.*

Coach Wallace Honeycutt, Coach Joe Campbell, Pastor Scottie Smith, Tim Campbell, Ray Chandler, and Bob Moon... *You have provided defining moments which have shaped my trajectory in life. I'm forever grateful.*

Contents

PREFACE

It's been a year since this book grew out of a friendship and partnership with Promise Keepers. Like hundreds of thousands of other men, I have a "PK stadium story." It seems like just yesterday that I sat in those stands, but the ministry today is equally compelling. For almost twenty years, this group of men and women has been committed to the unified goal of seeing "men transformed worldwide." That's a goal worthy of the investment of a life, so I was honored when Promise Keepers ask me to write a book that would speak to men about the issues of living a life of *adventure, challenge,* and *significance*...a life of faith at full speed.

Books are funny things. You pour your heart out onto the pages, rush them to the printer, and then watch them leave the arenas in the hands of thousands of men. What personal discoveries await them? How might God use the words to change hearts that can change families that can change communities? You never know for sure. Books are like little time bombs—you never know when they might "go off" in someone's life.

I know that some of the books have exploded in the lives of friends who gave them to friends who were looking for truth... and found the book served as a starting point for eternal conversations. I know of a friend in particular who buried his mom this year and is wrestling through the hard *why* questions...and who found some answers and plenty of empathy from someone who has "been there."

One Shot

And then there is the way the book has affected me and my little tribe. You have heard it said that "life imitates art"; well, this book was a *real* preface in my life and my wife's life as we heeded our calling to "live a life of faith at full speed." As the parents of three rambunctious boys, we are accustomed to energy and adventure. In the last several months—in addition to the normal journey—I have left my salaried position of sixteen years and ventured out on our own (translation: no more paycheck; working out of the spare bedroom). We certainly love the adventure... on most days.

In the midst of changing jobs, I jumped into working on a presidential campaign in Iowa, navigating the dizzying world of politics for several months. And—oh yes—our fourth baby (a girl) was just born a few weeks ago.

When we first found out that the stork was descending again, my three boys came to me as a team and jointly requested permission to make a prayer request. (I can tell you that my young sons are almost always working toward their own—usually conflicting—agendas.) To see them unified—even the two-year-old standing at attention alongside his brothers—meant that this was a serious meeting for them. My oldest son spoke for the group: "Dad, we want to ask God for something."

Sure, I thought. *Asking God is the best place to start. But...this is a six-, five-, and two-year-old; they aren't praying for the peace of Jerusalem, they're praying for things like a dog or permission to carry a lizard to school.* "Yeeeessssss?" I said, "What do you want to ask the Lord about?"

"We have enough boys in the house," he responded. "We want a girl baby. Is that okay?"

14

PREFACE

So, like a good judge quizzing the jurors, I asked, "Is this what you all want?" Each one, including the two-year-old (obviously coached), all nodded his head "yes." Now, when people congratulate us on the birth of our daughter, the boys have this great sense of accomplishment because, as they say, "God made her a girl because we asked Him."

Yes, it's been quite a year—and the year ahead shows no signs of slowing down. By the time you read this, our daughter will be in our arms as well as in our hearts; we will know if business visions become reality or were just dreams. All I know for sure is that time waits for no one. When we see the lives of our children, whether they are young or have children of their own, we see time moving forward. It is a great reminder that to some extent we are being replaced by our children.

The Greeks had an interesting practice. They didn't write eulogies; they simply asked one question of a person's life: *Did the person live with passion?* And so it is with us. Does your life have the adventure, challenge, and significance that you were designed to experience? Does your life mean something? Does it matter?

No matter what juncture of life you are in, it's easy to recognize that life is fragile and finite. We get one shot at it, and the question must be asked, year after year, moment by moment: "Am I living it with passion?"

In these pages, I hope you find the fuel to go full speed.

—*Todd Burkhalter,*
April 2008

INTRODUCTION

We have one shot at this life.
One shot to make life count.

THE BIBLE SAYS THAT LIFE IS like a vapor: "[It] *appears for a little while and then vanishes*" (James 4:14). Your life is like a field goal attempt at the end of the final game of the season. You get one shot at it. Just one.

We must feel and know this truth in the depths of our hearts. If not, we risk wasting our lives—truly wasting them. God designed life to be lived with purpose, passion, and direction. The shot must mean something; it needs to count for something.

The game of life is playing out all around us, and the pressure never seems to let up: bills to pay, places to go, things to do, a job that demands our commitment and time....We try to find balance in the chaos of our lives at home: kids to feed, things to fix, and, of course, the life experiences we share with our wives. If we aren't careful, the moment by moment demands of the days quickly turn into weeks, the weeks into years, the years into decades, and then, before we know it, a lifetime evaporates…*and the chance at taking our best shot could pass us by.* That would be a waste.

Let's take a pregame walk-through in the next few minutes: catch our breath together, get some answers, get some perspective on the game so far, and make some adjustments as we consider the rest of the game. God is the owner, coach, and QB of the team. He knows what's going on. He sees the big picture; He knows the blood, sweat, and tears of life on the field. He comes into the huddle of our life as if to say, "Everybody take a breath. We are going to win. Here's the play. Here's what we're doing. Men, here's your *purpose.*"

In the pages ahead, we will listen to what He is telling us through His Word and His Spirit. We'll examine the lives of men like Caleb and Paul who put it all on the line for a higher cause. You'll meet men whom I respect—men who have risked it all on the promises of God. Together, we will search out the answers to life's most vital questions:

- What is truth?
- How do I discover the heart of God?
- Who am I? What do I believe?
- What is true life?
- How do I die to my old life?
- How do I risk everything on the promises of God?
- How do I connect with the men and women most important to me?
- What does it really mean to live a life of adventure, challenge, and significance—a life of faith at full speed?

Old ideas may be challenged. New ways will be considered. The answers have the potential to drastically change the way you approach life and play the game. Stepping out and living life at full speed is an adventure—sometimes even a dangerous one—so at the end of each chapter, you will *assess* those risks, *consider* them in light of God's promises, and then *choose* to take your one shot at making life count.

I'd highly recommend that you huddle up with a few men. You'll even find some thought provoking questions along the way to keep your team thinking and talking. So, if possible, get shoulder to shoulder with a few other men and read this book together. Huddle up with a few guys who can encourage you, support you, and speak into your life. Ultimately, this is our locker room. As individuals, we become part of something bigger than our own goals. As a team, we go forward, committed to one other, playing for a higher calling.

While some try to avoid risk, we choose to embrace it as an essential part of a man's being. We have a passion for the unknown. We have an internal drive to push beyond what has been explored, beyond what we can do, beyond what we can see. We were made for the adventure—created for a life lived with unashamed passion.

True risk always begins in the heart. It begins by understanding who we are in Jesus Christ and who He is in us. With a practical and passionate understanding of what God has *already* done, everything you are and everything you do finds its place. The apostle Paul called this "the great mystery of the faith." This mystery brings clarity back into the game.

God's ways are deeper than the ocean and higher than the night stars. He is infinite, beyond our greatest imagination. As we listen to Him speak in the huddle, old words will become new. Everyday concepts become extraordinary. As we listen carefully to His plan, we see Him redefining the fundamentals of the game. This is the power of God; this is where passion starts and purpose comes into focus. This is where we discover *adventure, challenge, and significance: a life of faith at full speed.*

In 1 Corinthians 16:13–14, the apostle Paul declared, *"Be on your guard; stand firm in the faith; be men of courage; be strong. Do everything in love."* That is the battle cry that we take with us as we seek to discover the challenge, significance, and adventure of a Promise Keeper. Don't hold back. Get your head in the game and focus through all nine chapters. Be there in the end. Be there with the guys in your huddle. Do this because you only have one shot at this life…

One shot to make it count.

Just one.

Choose well.

Live by faith.

Go full speed.

SECTION I
ADVENTURE

Adventure (ād-vĕn'chər) *n.* An undertaking of a hazardous nature; a risky enterprise. 2. An unusual experience or course of events marked by excitement and suspense.

One Shot *begins with a sense of adventure, and the adventure begins with a heartfelt quest to understand the source of truth, the heart of God, and who we are as sons of God the Father. This is where the adventure begins, where risk is realized, and where the great journey is launched.*

Life is either a great adventure, or it is nothing at all.

—*Sir Edmund Hillary,*
the first man to climb Mt. Everest

Truth is tough. It will not break, like a bubble, at a touch; nay, you may kick it about all day, like a football, and it will be round and full at evening.

—*Mark Twain*

Who dares nothing, need hope for nothing.

—*Johann Friedrich von Schiller*

You can't cross the sea merely by standing and staring at the water.

—*Rabindranath Tagore*

Adventure is not outside man; it is within.

—*David Grayson*

You shall know the truth, and the truth shall set you free.

—*Jesus Christ,*
John 8:32

CHAPTER ONE

THE ADVENTURE OF TRUTH

TWO MEN STAND ONLY A FEW feet apart. Angry, shouting crowds are pressing in. Accusations fill the air. The Roman palace in Jerusalem has become a makeshift courtroom. Though He has been found guilty of no crime, the man on trial is moments away from being sentenced to death.

The two men face each other. One, the political son of Caesar. The other, the Son of a different King. One stands tall and powerful, robed and ringed by the most powerful political and military force in history. The other stands beaten and bloodied, mocked, questioned, and ridiculed by those around Him.

As the crowd surges, demanding blood, the distance between the men closes. One is torn by his allegiance to Rome and his desire to please the religious leadership of the land he occupies. The other stands unwavering, intent on His destiny, holding His course.

Therefore Pilate says to Him, "So you are a king?" Jesus answers, *"You are right in saying I am a king. In fact, for this reason I was born, and for this I came into the world, to testify to the truth. Everyone on the side of truth listens to me"* (John 18:37).

The man of Rome is trying desperately to find a way out of his predicament. Neither desiring to shed the blood of an innocent man, nor wishing to offend those he has been called to dominate, he comes to the end of his options in attempting to find a solution that will satisfy everyone.

The man of God is fully aware of His destiny and the road that lies before Him. His words are truth. They also reflect His intent to fulfill the purposes for which He came to earth as a man.

"What is truth?" Pilate asks (John 18:38), his words reflecting both his sincerity and his exasperation.

What is truth? The question is not just philosophical. Truth has enormous practical applications. Truth gives us our direction. Truth is our saving grace in a storm. Truth provides life-giving water to those who are thirsty.

Truth is reality.

Pilate is far from home, questioning his role in this Roman outpost. He would love to avoid the truth in the man before him, but the crowds continue to press in, their leaders stirring up demands and accusations against the man of God.

Pilate longs for truth, but, because of his position, he is unwilling to take a risk on truth as it is being revealed before him. The man of God is sentenced to death, fulfilling the prophecies of the how the Messiah would live and die. (See John 18:32.) Christ bows His head and is swept away by the angry mob.

A QUESTION OF TRUTH

What is "truth"? Truth is a question of life or death, light or darkness, fulfillment or futility. Truth is a matter of unavoidable importance to men who know that they only have one shot at making life count. Find truth, and you find the way. If you don't find truth, you wander listlessly in your quest, randomly and without direction, stumbling without aim. Discovering truth is where the adventure must begin.

It takes a man of great courage to ask what truth is. It takes a man of great faith to accept truth when he finds it. But the question of Pontius Pilate still remains: What *is* truth?

Throughout history, truth has been defined in a number of different ways. Some of these definitions have lasted throughout the centuries. Others are relatively new, extensions of this age in our culture.

> Ask some of your friends, "What is truth? Is truth absolute?" See how they respond. Make a mental note of the different answers you hear.

The Oppressive Regime: Truth through Power

Through the ages—and even today—"truth" has been dictated by oppressive governments. Half of the world's population lives under some form of oppressive regime or police state. These states tout a collective ideology or set of laws that define their cultural truth. These regimes allow no variation from the state's position. Proclaiming anything other than the state's truth can be life threatening.

The Supreme Right of Kings: Truth through Royalty

There was a time when people believed that God spoke directly through earthly kings. What the king did and said was accepted as the word of God. As the king spoke, so spoke the Almighty. His words were accepted as truth from on high, and he often assumed total control over the church.

The Authority of the Religious Elite:
Truth through the Dictates and Mandates of Spiritual Leaders

For many, "truth" is defined by the doctrines or teachings of religious leaders. Their proclamations and ideas are considered to be absolute truth from God. Many accept these religious cults and their edicts over the written Word of God, and Scripture is often used to justify their teachings and leadership.

The Whims and Peer Pressures of Society:
Truth through the Masses

Often, people just go with the flow, never wondering if what their culture is saying is true. Majority rules, fads come and go, and undiscerning individuals are swept along for the ride.

The Opinion of the Individual:
Truth through Personal Estimation

In the world, truth is "relative." What is true for me may not be true for you. Truth varies according to circumstances and your personal understanding. Today in our culture, the suggestion of "absolute truth" (an unwavering constant that never changes) is considered arrogant, uninformed, and naïve.

The struggle to define truth continues. There is the desire in each of us to define our own reality, choose our own course, and live independent of any absolute truth—besides the one we create for ourselves.

THE ADVENTURE FOR TRUTH IN SCRIPTURE

Sometimes the adventure of truth begins with the adventure of *finding* truth. Such is the story of Bob Cornuke. He is a former police investigator and SWAT team member. Now he seeks to discover the heart of God and show the historical evidence for

God's truth in the Bible. Bob's life is an ongoing quest for truth that has taken him into some of the most remote and dangerous corners of the globe. Using the Bible as the sole guide for his expeditions, he has been shaking up the assumptions of archeological and geographical scholars with his findings.

Seeking truth at this level has its own set of risks. In 1988, for example, Bob ventured into Saudi Arabia to photograph Mt. Sinai. Using "creative means" to enter this heavily protected and sacred Muslim enclave, Bob and his team faced continual danger.

His quest for truth has turned into an adventure of its own, taking him on a journey filled with danger and risk. His findings cause any curious mind to contemplate the historical truth of biblical stories and events that some have deemed to be myth or fable. Bob chronicles his adventures and the conclusions of his search in the books *Ark Fever* and *Relic Quest*.

Our intense desire to find truth should be as intense as Bob Cornuke's adventure—because truth is that important. If the Bible contains the very words of God, if Scripture is historically accurate and spiritually illuminating, then we have discovered truth itself.

The adventure of discovering truth, therefore, is found in the quest for taking God at His word. In order to begin this quest, we must be willing to leave behind conventional religious thought. The world of religion and the teachings of some churches make the Bible seem...well, less than absolute truth.

> **If you really believed that the words of God, as recorded in the Bible, were absolute truth, how would that change the way that you live, think, and act?**

ONE SHOT

Some people associate God's Word with outdated laws. To many, the Bible feels outdated and hard to understand. Some feel that it limits our creativity and abilities to explore an adventurous life. Many believe that Scripture puts a leash on our desires and abilities to do the things that are important to us. On top of that, they ask, haven't the Scriptures been used for centuries to oppress, dictate, repress, and discourage those who seek inspiration and support?

Nothing could be further from God's intention. Actually, the Bible says that, *"Where the Spirit of the Lord is, there is freedom"* (2 Corinthians 3:17). *"Anyone who examines this evidence will come to stake his life on this: that God himself is the truth"* (John 3:33 MSG).

If that's a little hard for you to believe, there's a good chance that you represent one of two extremes when it comes to your beliefs about the Bible. On one hand, you might have grown up with the Word of God; it feels commonplace and irrelevant. You would open up its dusty pages for yourself, but the teachings you have heard from the Bible sound contrary to the passions of your heart.

On the other hand, perhaps the Bible has never been part of your heritage. Perhaps you think the Bible is nothing more than myths and fables passed down through an old worn-out religion.

But what if you're missing out? What if the Bible is true and *alive*? What if God's Word contains a different message from the one you've heard all these years? What if you've misread both His heart and the instruction that He has given us in the Bible?

What if the truth of Scripture actually leads us to freedom? To adventure? To challenge? To significance? What if the words of Scripture free us from the lies of the world? What if the truths in Scripture actually free us from the very things that we negatively associate with the Bible—things like pressure, judgment, bondage, and a deep, burdensome sense of guilt and obligation? Psalm 119:32 says, *"I run in the path of your commands, for you have set my heart free."* If the Bible is really about freedom, then most men would be willing to take a risk with a book like that.

Each man must search for this kind of truth on his own. This is a noble search—one that the Bible itself encourages. The search may not take you to the far reaches of the globe like Bob Cornuke, but the issues are ones that each man must seek answers for. There are many fascinating books on this topic written by those who have investigated the possibility that the Bible is accurate, alive, and truthful. (Some of these books are listed in the resource section at the end of this book.)

If you have doubts, it might take some time and effort to get your questions answered. Many men have asked difficult questions and found satisfying answers. They have found the Bible to be a brilliant ray of truth in a dark world.

The Bible is also the road map for an incredible adventure. It calls us to break out of the mold that the world tries to force us into. It tells us that we can be free from harmful desires and impulsive instincts that lock us into the shackles of sin.

The Bible itself calls us to a life of freedom—a life of excelling, a life of adventure—that leads to things we can only dream of. Through Scripture, we get the ultimate bird's eye view of our situation and condition. The Bible certainly works like a compass showing us where "true north" is, but it's more than that: the complexity and the diversity of Scripture works like a GPS. I'm not great with directions, so every time I rent a car I get a "Never Lost" GPS. The device uses signals from satellites to calculate my exact location and gives me directions to where I want to go. It gives me multiple points of reference and then displays all the information in vibrant color and 3-D graphics. Scripture does the same thing. It shows us where we are, where we want to be, and it illuminates the path to get there. Every step of the way is an adventure—an adventure for truth.

Pontius Pilate asked, "*What is truth?*" (John 18:38). History, archaeology, and the Bible give the answer: "*The sum of Your word is truth, and every one of Your righteous ordinances is everlasting*" (Psalm 119:160 NASB).

THE ADVENTURE FOR TRUTH IN JESUS CHRIST

Sometimes the truth can be painful—really painful. Nowhere is this more obvious than in the world of music. If you've ever watched *American Idol*, you know exactly what I'm talking about. The contestants seem to be sincere people, and they all sincerely believe they can sing. When they realize the truth, it really hurts.

I've been in the music industry for nearly a decade, working with record labels and artists. I have found that even an artist who *can* really sing often finds performing painful—even when he or she is singing in church. In a service years ago, I witnessed the most agonizing singing experience ever…and unfortunately, I was a part of it.

It was youth Sunday—a chance for the teens to share their God-given talents with the adults. We led worship, preached the sermon, and—you guessed it—sang. I was supposed to sing a duet with one of my friends. We were doing an old Bill Gaither tune; the chorus went, "Jesus, Jesus, Jesus, there's just something about that name." But a little mishap during a football game on Friday night had left me short one tooth and long on one big fat lip. "Jethuth, Jethuth, Jethuth" just wouldn't do. My friend, a fifteen-year-old with a rich, baritone voice, decided to go solo.

"What's the worst thing that could happen?" he asked as we waited behind a platform for his turn to sing.

"I guess you could mess up the words," I said.

"Yeah, I guess I could sing 'There is just *nothing* about that name,'" he laughed nervously.

At that point, we should have felt it coming. We should have prayed. We should have rebuked the demons of musical mischief. We should have run for our car in the parking lot, headed for the mountains, and never returned. Instead, we walked on stage…I to the piano and he to the microphone. (To protect my friend from further pain, I'm going to call him "Alex." It would only add to his embarrassment if I called him by his real name, Rob Bright.)

My fingers began to play a beautiful introduction, and Alex's voice began to fill the sanctuary: "Jesus, Jesus, Jesus, there's just nothing about that name…." I flinched. *Did he really just sing "nothing"?* The people in the congregation didn't seem to notice anything, though the deacon sitting to our right cocked his head slightly to the side. Had I heard it wrong? *No reason for concern*, I thought. *He has two more chances to do it right.*

"Jesus, Jesus, Jesus, there's just nnnnnothing about that name." This time the congregation began to fidget, and a few whispered to each other. The gray hairs of the old ladies in the front pew momentarily stood on end. *Certainly that was a fluke*, I thought. But as we head towards the final chorus, beads of sweat began to form on Alex's forehead. I checked for the location of the nearest exit. *Dang, too far to crawl without being noticed.*

Note by note, the chorus approached again—like a freight train out of control, headed for a sharp corner on the edge of the steep cliff. Alex was holding on to the edge of the pulpit, knuckles white, trying to keep from passing out. He took one last breath as he reached the crescendo of the final words of that sacred song: "There's just…ssnnnssnothing about that name."

I played the final chord of the song; it dissipated into silence. Someone clapped a little. A few others joined in—kind of like the clapping of golf spectators when a pro misses a six inch putt. Alex's head dropped to the podium and tears began to fall. After an awkward eternity, the pastor came up to the pulpit and put his arm around him. "Alex, you believe that there is *something* about the name of Jesus, don't you?"

"Yes, yes, yes," Alex chokes out.

Ouch. Pain. We really hurt for him, but that hasn't stopped us from retelling the story at every church reunion over the last three decades.

SOMETHING ABOUT THE NAME

The fact is that there *is* something about that name—the name of Jesus—because there's something unique about Jesus Himself, something that cannot be overlooked by a man who is honestly seeking truth.

Christ was recognized as a great teacher, as one who knew the right thing to do in difficult situations. Individuals came to Him secretly in the night and followed Him by the thousands during the day. In each situation, they were seeking the truth He possessed.

THE ADVENTURE FOR TRUTH

Shortly before Jesus was crucified, He pulled together his disciples, explaining to them what was going to happen in the days that followed. He told these friends that He was going to the Father. *"Thomas said to him, 'Lord, we don't know where you are going, so how can we know the way?'"* (John 14:5).

Jesus' answer was simple—and baffling. Even today it is confounding. Jesus not only claimed to *know* the truth and *know* the way to the Father, but He also said, *"I **am** the way and the truth"* (John 14:6, emphasis added).

The adventure for truth, then, is not only the adventure of finding out what is right and wrong, *it's the adventure of discovering a person—the person of Jesus Christ.* You have to think about this deeply. Christ's claim must be taken seriously, pondered, evaluated, and eventually responded to. Either this man was crazy, or He is who He said...and each of us must answer this question in our own minds.

Our search for truth can never be complete until we find Him. Anyone who sets off on the adventure for truth must eventually deal with the person of Jesus Christ, for He said that He *is* the truth that we seek.

Jesus Christ is real. His presence is not just a theological concept; it is a present *reality.* Faith in Christ is not "faith based fantasy." It's not a "belief system." He is real whether we believe in Him or not...and if He is who He claimed to be, we reject Him at great expense. If we accept His presence and His truth in everyday living, it changes everything.

> **What if truth is a person? How would that affect the way you search for truth and the way that you find truth?**

Truth, then, is ultimately found in God's Word and through a personal relationship with Jesus Christ. This one-two punch of truth gives us a clear bearing. With this sense of direction, we can find our place and navigate through the difficulties and the struggles before us. With a firm standard of truth and a dynamic relationship with Jesus Christ, life is anything but predictable. It becomes an adventure.

The principles of Scripture give you absolutes that you can use to check your position and direction. In the Bible, Jesus calls us to follow...and His path is never predictable. He wasn't the kind of person who followed the beaten path. He blasted through the expectations that people had for Him as a Jewish teacher. He lived by an authority that was higher than the religious establishment. When He came face-to-face with political authorities, He made it clear that He lived by a different standard. *"My kingdom is not of this world,"* he told Pilate (John 18:36).

THE ADVENTURE BEGINS

Like Pilate, we must come face-to-face with the truth of Jesus Christ. Like Pilate, we must choose what we will do with Him and His Word. The crowds pressure us to deny Him and reject Him, but something inside tells us to seek Him and find Him with our whole heart. It is a risky choice. Risk is part of any true adventure. The adventure for truth is no exception.

Count the cost, assess the risks, and seriously consider joining the adventure...because there is such a thing as truth, because truth matters, and because truth can be found through God's Word and in Jesus Christ.

RISK ASSESSMENT

► Do you have questions or doubts about the authority and accuracy of the Bible? Are you willing to take the time and effort to answer those doubts?

► If Jesus is *"the way and the truth and the life"* as He claims (John 14:6), what holds you back from living, believing, and trusting in Him as your source of truth?

► Where does your truth come from right now? Parents? Traditions? Emotions? Friends? Professors? What would you need to change if you made God's Word and Jesus Christ your primary sources of truth?

THE REWARDS OF RISK

▶ **Psalm 51:6**

What you're after is truth from the inside out. Enter me, then; conceive a new, true life.

▶ **John 7:24**

Don't be nitpickers; use your head—and heart!—to discern what is right, to test what is authentically right.

▶ **2 Timothy 3:16**

Every part of Scripture is God-breathed and useful one way or another—showing us truth, exposing our rebellion, correcting our mistakes, training us to live God's way.

▶ **John 8:32**

You will experience for yourselves the truth, and the truth will free you.

THE ADVENTURE FOR TRUTH

TAKING A RISK ON THE TRUTH

Changing your sources of truth is a milestone that will alter the course of your life. In ancient times, when people made significant decisions that would alter their courses, they sometimes made large piles of rocks (called *cairns*) as remembrances of life-altering events.

If you have changed your source of truth today, create something that will serve as a reminder to you and others of your decision. Be creative with this. Make it personal and make it lasting.

Dear God, I want the emptiness in me to be filled with the knowledge of Jesus Christ and the truth about Him. Lord, I believe. Help my unbelief when I struggle to believe You and Your Word. Allow me to understand Scripture and have a desire to study it. I want the peace and freedom that Jesus gives. In Jesus' name, amen.

The music that really turns me on is either running toward God or away from God. Both recognize the pivot, that God is at the center of the jaunt.

—*Bono*

We must try to speak of His love. All Christians have tried, but none have done it very well. I can no more do justice to that awesome and wonder filled theme than a child can grasp a star. Still…as I stretch my heart toward the high, shining love of God, someone who has not before known about it may be encouraged to look up and have hope.

—*A. W. Tozer,*
Knowledge of the Holy

As we acquire more knowledge, things do not become more comprehensible but more mysterious.

—*Albert Schweitzer*

God writes the gospel not in the Bible alone but also on trees and in the flowers and clouds and stars.

—*Martin Luther*

CHAPTER 2

I'M A SAILOR AT HEART, AND ALL sailors respect the fact that the sea is vast and encompassing. Each time they set sail, they know the risk. At night they see the stars reflected in the water, and during the day they look down into the deep. The experienced sailors I know have great respect—even awe—for the sea.

I'm a follower of Christ, but I can never fully understand the vastness of the heart of God. Men of faith all know the same thing, and they respect the fact that the depths of God's heart are far beyond them. Each time they set off to discover the heart of God, they know that they are taking a risk, yet they are continually drawn to the challenge of discovery.

For a lifetime they skim across the surface of His greatness, experiencing the love of God but never able to adequately explain it. Some are highly educated and overly pretentious, claiming they can contain God in a doctrinal statement or a list of attributes. But those who have tasted the goodness of the Lord set off to discover His heart with respect, awe, and wonder.

WELCOME TO THE ADVENTURE

If God exists, there can be nothing more important than discovering Him and His heart. Nothing. Nothing more important than embarking on this adventure. If He exists, God is absolutely central to our existence. He alone holds the keys to the meaning of life. Without an awareness of Him, our existence would be little more than random, unconnected events that add up to nothing.

Discovering His heart, therefore, is an adventure—a calling of the highest order. The quest requires sweat, guts, and tears. Discovering the heart of God requires that we search our hearts—and sometimes be disturbed by what we find.

When we discover His strength, we realize our own weaknesses. When we catch a drop of His wisdom, we realize the ocean of our own ignorance. The search for the heart of God is an adventure like none other. It must begin today—and every day—and will follow us into eternity.

God is God. We are not. God is the God of all, the Lord of all, the Master of all...including us. And this is where the risk comes in. The one who seeks God risks it all. The adventure to discover Him never ends, and we will be changed through the search.

IN THE BEGINNING

"*In the beginning God created the heavens and the earth*" (Genesis 1:1). That's the way it all began. At one moment there was nothing; then God spoke, and *bam!*—it was. No man has ever offered a better explanation for the origin of matter. Even those who believe in the Big Bang Theory admit that something must have caused it. We know from physics and simple logic that something never emerges from nothing. Because there is something (matter), it must have had a first cause.

The universe stands as a testimony to God's greatness and existence. Nature is a reflection of His intricate design. This may be one of the reasons that men are continually drawn back to the wilderness. With a backpack and a sleeping bag, we have all the tools we need to see the fingerprints of God.

I remember sailing out of port on a beautiful New England fall day. My wife and I had been longing to get away. We looked forward to our time together, exploring islands off the coast of Maine. As we prepared to drop anchor in the late afternoon, the majesty of fall in New England was in full array. Isaiah 11:9 was never so true: *"The earth will be full of the knowledge of the LORD as the waters cover the sea."* It was fabulous, energizing, and confirming. If we are willing to look up, look around, and think about it for awhile…God becomes so obvious.

Do you think most men want to discover God and His heart? Why or why not?

In the book of Job, God points to His creation as evidence of His character and power:

> *Brace yourself like a man; I will question you, and you shall answer me. Where were you when I laid the earth's foundation? Tell me, if you understand. Who marked off its dimensions? Surely you know! Who stretched a measuring line across it?* (Job 38:3–5)

For three chapters, God uses example after example from nature as evidence of his wisdom and his authority. How did this affect Job? Though he had endured great suffering, he bowed his knee before the heart of God.

In Psalm 14:1, David said, *"The fool says in his heart, 'There is no God.'"* *"God"* is the only explanation for the existence of anything. Paul wrote, *"For since the creation of the world God's invisible qualities—his eternal power and divine nature—have been clearly seen, being understood from what has been made, so that men are without excuse"* (Romans 1:20).

But can the heart of this God be known?

GOD REVEALED

God reveals Himself through nature. That's obvious. Creation gives us a general awareness of the existence and work of the Creator. David sang, *"The heavens declare the glory of God; the skies proclaim the work of his hands"* (Psalm 19:1). We can see evidence of a Creator by analyzing the things that the Creator has made. But in order to know what the heart of the Creator is like, we need to have something more than what we can see or feel in the material world.

At this point we must take up the adventure for truth. What is the truth about God? We know that the answers lie within the sources of truth that God has given us: the Word of God and Jesus Christ. Through these two pillars of truth, we learn many things about God because He uses these things to speak directly to us about Himself.

For one thing, Scripture shows us that God was the original "Promise Keeper." The writer of Hebrews says, *"When God made the promise to Abraham, since He could swear by no one greater, He swore by Himself"* (Hebrews 6:13 NASB). God swore to keep His promise. Nobody can change it. God's promises and purposes cannot be altered. God's ministry cannot be derailed. If He ever broke His word, the universe would fall apart.

The Adventure to Discover the Heart of God

From the Bible, we also discover that God is personal: *"For you created my inmost being; you knit me together in my mother's womb"* (Psalm 139:13).

I think this is absolutely amazing. I don't think it's amazing that God *can* do these things or that He *did* do these things. I think it's amazing that He *wanted* to create us. It's stunning actually. Think about it for a moment or two and you will begin to enter into the mystery of the heart of God. He has no need; He has no lack. What could God possibly gain by creating us? Could it be that He simply did it for His glory and pleasure...and for our benefit?

It's through questions like these that we begin to touch the surface of the meaning and the passion for which we were created. Many men assume that living a spiritual life means living an emasculated life—a life void of adventure. Nothing could be further from the truth. Man was made in the image of God and came from the hand and heart of God. If God created us as a gift, then a passive, passionless life is far from His design.

Long before your parents met, at the outset of creation, God planned for you...not quite in the same way expecting parents plan for a new arrival, though. His plan involved your very design. It was done with great loving care.

"Even the very hairs of your head are all numbered" (Matthew 10:30). No doubt about it: God is personal.

The fact that He created us proves it. The way He created us proves it. He created us with an empty space inside that only He can fill. Unless we know Him, we are basically empty. When exposed to His presence, the emptiness in us begins to cry out. And it doesn't matter what language you speak or what culture you're a part of or what religious background you come from—when His presence comes near, the emptiness inside you cries out to be filled.

I love all kinds of music, but I really enjoy classic rock and roll. ("Classic," of course, is just a nice way of saying that the songs are old and so are the people who listen to them.) In the *Behind the Music* series, VH1 follows the lives of the guys in the bands that we loved as kids—those who made it to the pinnacle of success. Back then they had it all: the fame, hit songs, the girls, and piles of money. But most of the stories end the same way. Twenty years later, many of these guys are still searching, disillusioned, and totally empty inside. It was a wild ride, but the core of it was totally void of any value or meaning.

> **In the past, what have you used to try to fill the emptiness in your life?**

We have a built-in hunger that makes our hearts long for God; we taste and feel our need for Him. Not even "sex, drugs, and rock 'n' roll" can satisfy it. We thirst for love, and that desire is a clear extension of the fact that God is love. (See 1 John 4:8.) God doesn't just love; He says that He *is* love. The love He gives is radically different from any other kind of love. Theologians sometimes say that God's love is "unconditional." This means that His love and acceptance are not based on our performance or on any conditions that we must meet. Consider these words from J. I. Packer in *Knowing God*:

> It is staggering that God should love sinners; yet it is true. God loves creatures who have become unlovely and (one would have thought) unlovable....Love among men is awakened by something in the beloved, but the love of God is free,

spontaneous, unevoked, uncaused. God loves men because he has chosen to love them.[1]

God defines Himself as the perfect loving Father, always pursuing us and delighting in the works of our hands. In this love, we are inspired to discover the height, the depth, and the adventure of following God's call on our life.

The perfection of His love, however, is only one aspect of the perfection of His entire being. Some call this His "holiness." Holiness is difficult for us to understand because nothing is holy except God; there is nothing that compares to Him in this way. He's absolutely blameless, and He judges correctly in all He does. He doesn't grade on a curve; He can't let one slip up go by without responding. This is reflected in the prayer of Hannah: *"There is no one holy like the LORD; there is no one beside you; there is no rock like our God"* (1 Samuel 2:2).

Again, this is where the quest to discover the heart of God must expand beyond our ability to compare Him to anything that we know or understand in the physical realm. There simply is nothing like God when it comes to His perfection. This should give us cause to proceed very carefully. If we seek the heart of God, we must realize that we are searching on holy ground— ground upon which we have no right to tread—so we must always search with awe, reverence, and complete humility.

Scripture reveals that God is perfectly holy...it also reveals that we clearly are not.

THE GREAT SEPARATION

Surely the arm of the LORD is not too short to save, nor his ear to dull to hear. But your iniquities have separated you from your God; your sins have hidden his face from you. (Isaiah 59:1–2)

Sin. This is the great barrier we face in our quest to discover the heart of God. We often think of ourselves in terms of others. *I didn't commit murder; I haven't committed adultery; I haven't done something terrible to anyone; I'm really not like all men; I have not done that much wrong in my life.* But we are wrong.

Our shortcomings—the things that we should do but don't, our direct disobedience to the commands of God, the independent spirit that makes us want to be the gods of our own lives—all these things are sin. They stretch out before us like the Grand Canyon, separating us from God. God says in His Word that *"all have sinned and fall short of the glory of God"* (Romans 3:23). That would include you and me.

Worse yet is the reality that there is nothing we can do to fix this. What are we going to do? Try to jump the canyon? It is the nature of the male ego to try to make it across on his own, even if it means trying to kick a four hundred yard field goal or swim across the Pacific Ocean. Men are wired to try and accomplish things, but, in this situation, we just can't—and it would be arrogant to think that we could.

We are completely and absolutely helpless. We can't save each other; we can't save the planet; we can't save ourselves. We are dependent on God for our next breath; certainly we are dependent on Him for our salvation. However, we are in a state of rebellion. We are described in the Bible as *"God's enemies"* (Romans 5:10); the condition is hopeless. We are complete only in our depravity. We cannot realize a place where we will ever do enough, say enough, or be enough to measure up to God's standard or earn His love. Only Jesus Christ was able to keep every one of God's commandments and laws. The rest of us are separated by sin, and the canyon between us and God is just too deep for us to cross...

But it turns out that the love of God is deeper still.

Very rarely will anyone die for a righteous man, though for a good man someone might possibly dare to die. But God demonstrates his own love for us in this: while we were still sinners, Christ died for us. (Romans 5:7–8)

To discover the heart of God—to see what it looks like in action—all you have to do is look to the cross. On that hot and dusty mound of dirt and rock outside of Jerusalem, Christ willingly gave His life for ours. He made the sacrifice so we could arrive at a home He prepared for us. (See John 14:2.) He took the punishment of our sins on Himself and became the bridge to cross the canyon made by sin. The blood that dripped from the nails on the cross paints a picture of the ferocious love of God.

"Greater love has no one than this, that he lay down his life for his friends" (John 15:13). A man—a perfect man—did this for us, and in that single act of sacrifice, He showed us the heart of God.

ALTERING THE COURSE OF THE ADVENTURE

At the cross, we come to an intersection that requires a change in the direction of our lives. Beginning in our inner soul, we must align our lives with the truth—not just the truth about God's heart, but about our hearts as well. We have one of two directions to choose: we can forge on in our own arrogance, self-righteousness, and perceived strength; or, we can humbly kneel before a loving, holy, present Father.

Our inability to acknowledge that we are sinners, our unwillingness to confess our need for forgiveness, and our transgressions against God as the Creator of all things are offenses that God will judge. His wrath will be on us. Apart from turning to God, there is no relationship. Apart from crying out to God and asking Him to forgive our personal effort, our own sense of right and wrong, and our desires to go our own way, we will surely die an eternal death.

If we continue to be unrepentant, we will remain enemies of God and shall receive His full wrath, which was poured upon His Son for our pardon. We will be eternally crushed and separated from God to live a life of literal hell in a place of permanent suffering—not because God lacks mercy but because of our unwillingness to respond and follow God's heart.

Can you pinpoint a time or season when your heart was drawn to the heart of God? Was there ever a point when His love became real to you?

You see, the core of every relationship is forgiveness. I am not talking about a heartfelt hug-fest where we all sit around a campfire and say "someone offended me, but now I forgive him." I am talking about realizing that our lives have been lived apart from obedience and faith in Jesus Christ, and that it's time to be honest about that; it's time to adjust the way we approach the love of God.

You have to use your head on this one. Let's face it: God is God. We are not. Is there anything that we could do that might impress Him? Is there anything that we could do to make Him love us more? This is the deal: our shortcomings and our failures have caused separation between us and God. But *"if you confess with your mouth 'Jesus is Lord,' and believe in your heart that God raised him from the dead, you will be saved"* (Romans 10:9).

The Adventure to Discover the Heart of God

Two thousand years ago, Christ invaded this world with God's heart of love. God did not ask permission of anyone; He sent Jesus by His own initiative. He said, *"Repent, for the kingdom of heaven is near"* (Matthew 4:17).

Today, He is simply saying to each of us, *"Follow me"* (Matthew 4:19). As you begin to discover His heart, turn from your own way and receive new life—the life He brings.

RISKING IT ALL ON THE HEART OF GOD

God is beyond our understanding, and following Him requires a trust in His heart. It is more than just taking outward risks; it is more than just obedience. By God's design, our outward actions are supposed to come from an inner level of trust in His goodness.

At the center of God's heart is His Son and the promise that we are to be heirs with Christ. In John 17:22–23, Christ prayed, *"I have given them the glory that you gave me, that they may be one as we are one: I in them and you in me. May they be brought to complete unity to let the world know that you sent me **and have loved them even as you have loved me**"* (emphasis added).

It is a risk of faith to believe in the perfect love of God. It is a step of faith to believe God is pleased with us and even proud of who we have become when we turn in His direction. Every once in awhile, I get a glimpse of what God might be feeling toward me when I experience those powerful emotions for my sons. My young sons will never remember learning how to walk or speak, but I have hours of them doing both on videotape. I take delight—sheer delight—in watching them grow and learn. It's the same with God the Father. As we are learning His ways, He takes great delight in us as His sons.

It was I who taught Ephraim to walk, taking them by the arms; but they did not realize it was I who healed them. I led them with cords of human kindness, with ties of love; I lifted the yoke from their neck and bent down to feed them. (Hosea 11:3–4)

The LORD your God is with you, he is mighty to save. He will take great delight in you; he will quiet you with his love; he will rejoice over you with singing. (Zephaniah 3:17)

When we turn in God's direction, we are identified as His sons. He did this with Israel, and He does it with us. He said, *"I am the God of your father, the God of Abraham, the God of Isaac and the God of Jacob"* (Exodus 3:6). He's saying this in much the same way I might identify myself to my children's kindergarten teachers: "Hi, I am the father of Jackson, Christian, Bishop, and Holland." I am proud to be identified with my children. I am their father; I am responsible for them. I am responsible for protecting and providing for them and caring for their needs. I'm essentially saying to everyone, "Their care is in my hands."

How do you think your experience with your earthly father influences the way you think about God as a heavenly Father?

Unlike earthly fathers, however, God does this perfectly. We naturally draw parallels between our earthly fathers and God the Father. Part of the risk of faith is realizing this fact: regardless of your history, heartbreak, or parents, the relationship with Father God is like no other.

MAKING THE MOVE

Whether it is for the first time or the millionth time, I'm challenging you to begin the adventure and discover the heart of God on a personal level. It is the nature of any adventure to step into the unknown; the adventure to discover the heart of God is no exception. When you take the necessary step to align your path with the heart of God, you are launching out into the unknown. It's an adventure that has no equal because the greatness of God can never be understood in its entirety. It requires great humility and great courage to take such a step.

Taking this step will make you feel vulnerable; you will be stepping towards the One who knows you as you are. It's a tremendous risk because we are reaching out with the hope and anticipation that there is a God who will accept us and receive us as we are.

I believe God is calling call you to make that step...right now.

It's a step that must begin in your heart. It is not a call to some sort of radical outward change. It's not a commitment to change what you eat or what you drink or what you think or what you say. What God is calling you to is Himself. Nothing more—but certainly nothing less.

This is the great gospel of Jesus Christ. It is unlike anything else the world has ever known. Responding to this message is the way to start experiencing the heart of God on a personal level, which begins the lifelong adventure of daily rediscovery. In the process, you will also discover yourself, your meaning, and your purpose for living at all.

The apostle Paul prayed for us in this way:

My response is to get down on my knees before the Father, this magnificent Father who parcels out all heaven and earth. I ask him to strengthen you by his Spirit—not a brute strength but a glorious inner strength—that Christ will live in you as you open the door and invite him in. And I ask him that with both feet planted firmly on love, you'll be able to take in with all followers of Jesus the extravagant dimensions of Christ's love. Reach out and experience the breadth! Test its length! Plumb the depths! Rise to the heights! Live full lives, full in the fullness of God.

(Ephesians 3:14–19 MSG)

May that prayer be fulfilled in each of our lives as we begin the adventure of discovering the heart of God.

RISK ASSESSMENT

▶ What, in your opinion, would be the difference between knowing *about* the heart of God and actually *experiencing* His heart in a personal relationship?

▶ If you were to recognize God as God and turn control of your life over to Him, how might that change your life as it is right now?

▶ Are you willing to turn from your own life, confess your sins, and go in a new direction—toward God's heart for you?

THE REWARDS OF RISK

▶ **Romans 5:8**
But God put his love on the line for us by offering his Son in sacrificial death while we were of no use whatever to him.

▶ **1 Corinthians 2:7**
God's wisdom is something mysterious that goes deep into the interior of his purposes. You don't find it lying around on the surface. It's not the latest message, but more like the oldest— what God determined as the way to bring out his best in us, long before we ever arrived on the scene.

▶ **1 Peter 3:18**
For Christ died for sins, once and for all, the righteous for the unrighteous, to bring you to God.

▶ **John 1:12**
Yet to all who received him, to those who believed in his name, he gave the right to become the children of God. (NIV)

▶ **1 John 1:9**
If we confess our sins, he is faithful and just and will forgive us our sins and purify us from all unrighteousness. (NIV)

▶ **Revelation 3:20**
Here I am! I stand at the door and knock. If anyone hears my voice and opens the door, I will come in and eat with him, and he with me. (NIV)

The Adventure to Discover the Heart of God

▶ **Proverbs 3:5–6**

Trust God from the bottom of your heart; don't try to figure out everything on your own. Listen for God's voice in everything you do, everywhere you go; he's the one who will keep you on track.

▶ **Ephesians 1:11–12**

It's in Christ that we find out who we are and what we are living for. Long before we first heard of Christ and got our hopes up, he had his eye on us, had designs on us for glorious living, part of the overall purpose he is working out in everything and everyone.

TAKING A RISK ON DISCOVERING THE HEART OF GOD

Find a place where you can be alone. Ideally, find a place in a natural setting (like a lake, wooded area, or quiet space) or any other place where you can quietly consider God's wonders. As God confirms His presence through creation, ponder the verses above. Where is He leading you?

The Adventure to Discover the Heart of God

Father God, I know that all things revolve around You. I am certain of Your absolute control over the earth and the heavens. By Your mighty hand, all things happen. And yet, You have time for me. Thank You for listening to me when I pray. Thank You for sending Your Son Jesus. He lived the life I should have lived and died the death I should have died. In Jesus' name, amen.

Live your beliefs and you can turn the world around.

—*Henry David Thoreau*

In faith there is enough light for those who want to believe and enough shadows to blind those who don't.

—*Blaise Pascal*

One person with a belief is equal to a force of ninety-nine who have only interests.

—*John Stuart Mill*

What we need are more people who specialize in the impossible.

—*Theodore Roethke*

How does it feel to be on your own, with no direction home, like a complete unknown, like a rolling stone?

—*Bob Dylan*

For as [a man] *thinks in his heart, so is he.*

—*Proverbs 23:7* (NKJV)

CHAPTER 3

THE
ADVENTURE
OF BELIEF

I JUST MISSED THE 1960s. I MEAN, I was there, but I wasn't *really* there. I was just a kid; to experience the decade of the '60s in its glory, you had to be at least in your teens and ideally in your twenties. But even the people who were that age during the '60s aren't exactly sure what happened. Jefferson Airplane lead singer Grace Slick is credited with saying, "Anyone who says they remember the '60s wasn't really there."

Part of the revolution during those days, of course, had to do with music. The cultural chaos pushed music into an entirely different realm—a realm that had never been explored before. The Beatles, The Beach Boys, Jimi Hendrix...and a band called The Who.

Who was The Who? The Who wanted to be simply who they were, but I'm not sure they ever really figured out who that was. It seemed like they were always searching but never finding who they were supposed to be. One of their most famous songs actually came out in 1978, and it asked the same question of us that they asked of themselves. The song starts with a bold guitar chord progression: "da da da da BUM!...BA BUM! da da da da BUM!...BA BUM!" Very cool. Then comes the question: "Who are you; who are you? Who, who? Who, who?" If the needle on your record player got stuck at this point, the lyrics went like this: "Who, who? Who, who? Who, who? Who, who?...."

Let's just say that the '60s could be plenty confusing and a little annoying.

THE ULTIMATE QUESTION

The Who is now fading into musical history, but the question they asked in their classic song is still relevant: "Who are you?" It's a good question. How do you answer it? If someone asked you who you are, would you give him your name? Would you tell him what you do for a living? Would you explain what you do on your day off or tell him about your hobbies? Would you pull out your wallet and show him the picture on your driver's license? Would you tell him about your family, parents, grandparents, etc.?

If you ask an average guy on the street who he is, what criteria would he use to give you an answer?

Here's the question I'm asking you: *do you really know who you are?* And if you don't know, where will you go to find the answer?

THE ANSWER

The answer to that question really matters. What we believe about ourselves determines everything we do. Most people have that backwards. They think that what you *do* defines who you *are*, but it's really the other way around.

The Adventure of Belief

Let's ask the same question on a slightly different level. If someone asked you what a Christian is, how would you answer? Most answer the question with what Christians are supposed to *do*: they're supposed to go to church, read their Bibles, give money to charity…and they are supposed to be promise keepers. They're *not* supposed to drink, go to movies, swear, or be disagreeable with other people. Therefore, if you do—and don't do—certain things, most people will define you as a Christian. Does that answer really satisfy anyone?

Quite frankly, it doesn't satisfy me. It's too shallow; it doesn't go deep enough; it doesn't quench my thirst for a real answer.

To find a sufficient answer to such a critical question, we must embark on a different kind of adventure: *the adventure of belief.* The adventure begins where the road of truth and the heart of God intersect. It's where we discover our core identities as Christian men. During this never ending adventure of belief, we discover what we *do* believe and what we *should* believe. The true adventure begins as we face life with a clear perception of who we are and who we are to be.

I'm inviting you on such an adventure now…and my guess is that you will be very surprised—perhaps even shocked—about what you will find in God's Word.

THE ADVENTURE STARTS WITH GOD

When trying to figure out who we are, most of us try to define ourselves with outward things. We look at what we own, how much we are worth, where we live, what we do for a living, and so on. It becomes a big comparison game between ourselves and those around us.

Sometimes we see this get out of hand. We see fathers who try to define themselves by the performance of their children or men who are manic about their position or title. It's common to see people who ditch their responsibilities in order to pursue pleasure at almost any cost. Some travel the world trying to "find themselves," but, when they get there, they realize they are still stuck with the same question: *Who am I?*

If someone who knew you was asked who you are, how might he answer?

It often doesn't get any better inside the walls of the church. In fact, sometimes it's worse. The religious world is continually defining us by outward appearances and actions. Gordon England of Promise Keepers describes it this way:

> Typically, we'll hear a litany of how we've fallen short as men. It becomes a list of bad behaviors. The solution to that problem is usually not explained, but assumed by the man as 'clean up your act. Do better.' Kind of a self-help, behavior modification, a la psychobabble. That method sustains most men about three days. And most tragically, such an approach does not fit the Good News of Jesus Christ.[2]

Yes, the world and religion will always tell us that outward things define who we are on the inside.

The Bible says that's a lie.

As the One who created us, God alone has the authority to define who we are, clearly and accurately. More importantly, He sees beyond the things that we can see.

A great example of this is in 1 Samuel 16. At this point in history, Israel was in desperate need of a new king. Saul, the current king, had pretty much gone crazy with anger and disobedience. The prophet Samuel, after being clearly directed by God, went to Saul and stripped him of his authority as king. Then God sent Samuel on a mission to identify the next king of Israel, a man he knew God had already chosen. As Samuel arrived at Jesse's house, he assumed that Jesse's oldest son, Eliab, was the man. Perhaps Eliab was handsome or strong; maybe Samuel's assumption had something to do with Eliab being the oldest. We aren't told why, but something in Eliab's outward appearance or behavior made Samuel think he was the one. *"Surely the LORD's anointed stands here,"* Samuel thought (verse 6). And yet, the Lord said to Samuel:

> *Do not consider his appearance or his height, for I have rejected him. The LORD does not look at the things man looks at. Man looks at the outward appearance, but the LORD looks at the heart.* (1 Samuel 16:7)

"The LORD looks at the heart." He looks beneath the surface, past obvious outward physical things. God has never been fooled by outward appearances, never impressed by the things a man seems to be able to do. It's a heart issue, and God can see into the heart.

A MATTER OF THE HEART

To truly answer the question *Who am I?*, we must look beyond our self-perception. Certainly, we live with ourselves and know things about ourselves that no one else knows. But God knows us far better than we know ourselves. We must look beyond what we see and feel—beyond what the world and others tell us about

How would you describe yourself to a stranger? Would you use outward things, internal qualities, or some of both?

ourselves. We must turn to God for the answer. God and God's Word alone can tell us who we truly are, for only God looks beyond our outward appearances.

Who does God say you are?

If you've been immersed in the Christian world for any length of time, the words God uses to describe you may seem commonplace, redundant, and diluted. If you've never explored the Bible before, however, the words will sound unbelievable. As you seek to find the answer to the question, be warned that you are now exploring the mystery of the gospel; you're peeking into the infinite and beyond the astounding. God defines you at the very core of your being—your spirit. The adventure of belief will take you beyond what you think and feel is possible.

Who are you? To find out, you must discover four key aspects of your identity in Scripture.

1. Forgiven

You hear that word a lot: *forgiven*. Don't let it pass by this time without really thinking about it. If you've cried out to God in honesty and in surrender, confessed your sin, and responded to His love, you *are* forgiven. The penalty of the sin is gone—all of it.

Past sin, future sin, and the sin of the present? *Forgiven.* The lustful thoughts in your head? *Forgiven.* The moral failures? *Forgiven.* The lies you are living right now? *Forgiven.* You are forgiven for all the sins you will commit two years from now, two weeks from now, and two hours after reading this chapter. Forgiven!

In Romans 8:1–2, Paul proclaimed, *"There is now no condemnation for those who are in Christ Jesus, because through Christ Jesus the law of the Spirit of life set me free from the law of sin and death.*" That's not just good news, that's *very* good news...but it seems like so few believe it. At the same time, because we can trust God's leading, we can leave our hearts open to the Holy Spirit's conviction when we are hiding sin in our lives.

The world is filled with people working as hard as they can to try to pay for their sin. We are running around with a false sense of religious guilt that causes us to try to make ourselves worthy of God's forgiveness. It seems logical to try to pay God back for what He has done, because that's the way everything else works in the world. Even in church, it's common to hear things like this: "If God did all this for you, the least you can do for Him is...." But God's grace and love defy the logic of the world.

When Jesus died on the cross, He spoke a very unusual word: *Tetelestai.* (See John 19:30.) Though often translated *"it is finished,"* this is a Greek accounting word that literally means "it is paid in full." *Full.* Not partial; not a down payment that God made so we can pay the balance of forgiveness through our own efforts. No, He said, "paid in full." Through His death on the cross, Jesus absorbed the punishment of our sin—*all* of it.

The male ego and masculine pride interfere with our willingness to believe this. We like to think that *we* can fix things ourselves, or that *we* earn everything we have. But, quite frankly, we can't—not when it comes to God's forgiveness. It's done. It's finished. He paid for it all with His death. An awareness of what He has done—and the fact that we can never, ever, begin to repay it—should lead us into humble gratefulness and cause us to worship Him with a thankful heart.

2. Clean

The adventure to believe takes an interesting turn at this point. Is it possible for you to believe that you are actually clean? Scripture says that it's true, but are you willing to believe it?

At the core of our being, Jesus' death on the cross—the sacrifice—did a cleansing work. It wasn't symbolic. It wasn't partial. His cleansing was complete, and it was real beyond any earthly comparison. You might not feel clean, but are you willing to believe it because Scripture declares that it's true?

If we define self from the outside in, we will naturally conclude that our spirits are saturated with filth. That's not what God sees. He sees a spirit that is pure and powerful. The sacrifice made by Jesus on the cross has made you pure—without a speck or a flake of residue in your spirit—all in graphic contrast to the muck that clings to our flesh and our outward reputations. That's the truth.

> *If we confess our sins, [God] is faithful and just and will forgive us our sins and purify us from all unrighteousness.* (1 John 1:9)

> *"Come now, let us reason together," says the LORD. "Though your sins are like scarlet, they shall be as white as snow.* (Isaiah 1:18)

> *[Jesus] poured water into a basin and began to wash his disciples' feet, drying them with the towel that was wrapped around him.... "No," said Peter, "you shall never wash my feet." Jesus answered, "Unless I wash you, you have no part with me."* (John 13:5, 8)

3. Exchanged

In Ezekiel 36:25–27, God proclaimed a very interesting prophecy to His followers:

> *I will sprinkle clean water on you, and you will be clean; I will cleanse you from all your impurities and from all your idols. I will*

give you a new heart and put a new spirit in you; I will remove from you your heart of stone and give you a heart of flesh. And I will put my Spirit in you and move you to follow my decrees and be careful to keep my laws.

The fulfillment of this Old Testament prophecy is reflected throughout the New Testament. In 2 Corinthians 5:17–18, for example, Paul said, *"Therefore, if anyone is in Christ, he is a new creation; the old has gone, the new has come! All this is from God…."*

This is not theological jargon. This is where you must choose to enter into the adventure of belief. Remember that these things are true whether we believe them or not. Scripture tells us that things are not as they used to be…but do you believe it?

- You are no longer alive as you once were, even though familiar thoughts and emotions fill your soul; something was radically transformed when Christ came into your life.
- When you asked Jesus into your life, His Spirit actually came in.
- You were "born again" and have undergone a real spiritual rebirth at the core of your being.

Therefore, if anyone is in Christ, he is a new creation; the old has gone, the new has come!   (2 Corinthians 5:17)

4. Adopted

I have a friend who adopted a little girl from China. Her name is Lijuan, which means "beautiful and graceful." In parts of China, the law only allows each couple one child…and often girls aren't as prized as boys, so the orphanages are full of them. But now this little girl belongs. Now she is a daughter. Outwardly, it's not an obvious fit; but when it comes to the law, Lijuan is my friend's daughter, and my friend is her dad. The judges of the world declared it so; the legality of the agreement is binding forever, but the formal arrangement pales in contrast to the realities of their hearts.

Amazingly, my friend fell in love with his daughter before she even existed. They gave her a name; her room was painted pink; blankets and jammies were folded with care...all *months* before her conception—months before her world would label her "unwanted."

You see the parallel. It is part of the answer to the question, *Who are you?* Long before you felt the first sting of rejection from your world, God had given you a name and prepared a place in His heart for you. A new last name has been added to your name now: son of God. It is a legally binding change of identity. You might *feel* isolated from God; you might *feel* abandoned by Him; but it's not true. On the most important level—and in the most important relationship—you are secure, you are safe, and you are His, branded as a son of the King.

Are you willing to believe this?

NOT JUST THEOLOGY

*Forgiven, clean, exchanged, adopted by God...*these are not just theological terms. They are of immense practical value. If we could answer the question *Who are you?* with such truths, it would change everything.

First of all, having this understanding would give us an awareness of God's presence *in the midst* of the sin and temptation. No longer would we think falsely that sin could separate us from God as it could in the Old Testament.

The Adventure of Belief

We would recognize that God is our most important ally and our strength within our spirit—not just some distant helper we call in from the outside.

No longer would we use phrases such as "I walked away from God" or "I need to get back to Christ" because, in reality, if you are in Christ and He is in you, there could never be a separation—no matter how intense the sin and temptation seemed. Instead, we would remember His ongoing presence, rightfully claiming it as our own—just as we will always be the parents of our children.

In your opinion, does your belief determine what you do, or does what you do determine who you are?

When the Holy Spirit convicts us of sin, we would no longer instinctively try to run and hide from God like Adam and Eve did. We would know that it is not only *impossible* to hide from Him, but that there is no *need* to do so.

We would also naturally begin to resist temptation—not to *become* pure, but because we *are* pure...because He lives within us.

If you begin to answer the question of your identity with what Scripture says is true about you and choose to act on those truths whether you feel like it or not, the change will transform your life and give you an entirely new perspective.

This is the adventure of belief at its best! If you embrace the biblical fact that you are forgiven, clean, exchanged, and adopted, the possibilities are truly endless. By acting on these truths, you will revolutionize your marriage, your relationships with your children, and how you wrestle with temptations. By believing that what God says is true, the adventure of life takes off in fantastic new directions.

ALL ABOUT RELATIONSHIP

Let's consider what it means to serve and work beside God. This is a biggie. Many people believe that if they make a commitment to Jesus Christ, they will be drawn into some sort of religious forced work camp with an ugly employee-employer relationship where a judgmental God is always looking over their shoulder to see if they are producing enough, doing it in the right way, and not screwing up on the job. Christ totally redefined that; our "work" for God looks different. A group once approached Jesus and asked Him this question: *"What must we do to do the works God requires?"* (John 6:28). Jesus' answer was very revealing; it illuminates the key to the adventure of belief. *"The work of God is this: to believe in the one he has sent"* (verse 29).

True work for God is a matter of belief—not necessarily a specific action. In fact, the one who believes that what God says is true about him cannot help but serve God through actions. God has prepared work for us to do, and He is prepared to do it through us. We have the honor and the pleasure of doing it *with* Him.

Like every family along the Gulf coast, we had our share of storm damage from Hurricane Katrina. For days and weeks at a time, we worked beside our friends and neighbors to start the rebuilding process. My young sons were up most mornings ready to "work." Their first question of the day was usually, "How can I help?" or "Can I hammer today?" There was work to be done, but the completion of the work did not depend on my young children. It was my work to do. But I loved having them near me during the day, and they loved it too. It was my joy to let them hammer a few nails and hear them say, "Look what I've built for you."

The Adventure of Belief

As the Lord's children, let's face the fact that God really doesn't need our help. It's not like He has too much on His plate at any given time and needs us to help Him out. He is not dependent on us to complete His work. God is all-powerful, and He's all-present. This means that He has all the energy He needs to do anything He wants, and that He is everywhere He wants to be. God just doesn't need our help to get anything done. *"'My food,' said Jesus, 'is to do the will of him who sent me and to finish his work'"* (John 4:34).

What God desires, however, is *you*. And the heart of every man desires a real relationship with his heavenly Father. This mutual desire for each other transforms the "working" relationship between you and God into an adventure. If you believe that you're a child of God, a whole new scenario appears. It's as if God is calling out to us, saying, "Come enjoy some time with Me today," or, "Son, I want to show you how I do this work."

Not a single child would say "no" to such an offer. A father might actually place a hammer in the child's hand or allow him to use a saw. He may let him sit in on meetings or file papers; he may even ask for his child's input on important decisions. But let there be no question about who is actually doing the work or how the work is actually being completed.

The working relationship that you have with your heavenly Father is based on a *relationship first*, not your *performance of the job description*. The enemy of your soul will always challenge God's word here by telling you to settle for works—often even good works for God—instead of an abiding relationship with your Father in heaven. The devil will try to cast doubt on the unconditional love of God. Our adversary knows the struggle we all face in believing a love so glorious and good, so he often whispers through our doubts, saying things like: "No one could love you like that—certainly not God. You know Him; he's angry and demanding. He may be a King, but He's not a loving Father who enjoys your company and is proud of you. It's sacrilegious to even think of God like that…." In those moments, you have to choose whom you will believe: God's Word or the father of lies.

> *This resurrection life you received from God is not a timid, grave-tending life. It's adventurously expectant, greeting God with a childlike "What's next, Papa?"* (Romans 8:15 MSG)

In this context, "good works" simply become another father-son bonding opportunity, a chance to get to know your heavenly Father and see His heart for others more clearly. It's a chance to be mentored by the Creator of all things. You'll probably receive some satisfaction for your efforts. But be assured of the ultimate goal: as you spend time together, you will become more and more like the one who loves you and made you for Himself.

BACK TO THE QUESTION

Do you know who you are? The answer to that question really matters. Where will you go for the answer? Will you turn to God for the definition of truth or will you reference another source? Are you willing to begin the adventure of belief? Are you willing to embrace the spiritual truth that you are forgiven, clean, exchanged, and adopted?

Understanding who you are is critical, but, on top of that, if you ever happen to see The Who in concert and they sing, "Who are you?" you'll now be able to scream back an answer—and that's cool.

RISK ASSESSMENT

▶ Who are you? Write a brief description of yourself.

▶ Consider the four truths of who you are in your relationship with God (forgiven, clean, exchanged, adopted). Which of the four is the most difficult to believe and why?

▶ What outward standards does the world use to define you as valuable? What would happen if living up to those standards were no longer a priority for you?

▶ God's Word says that you are a son and not a slave to God. List five areas of your life that would immediately change if you really believed this. What risks would be involved in these changes?

THE REWARDS OF RISK

▶ **Romans 8:1**

Those who enter into Christ's being-here-for-us no longer have to live under a continuous low lying black cloud. A new power is in operation. The Spirit of life in Christ, like a strong wind, has magnificently cleared the air, freeing you from a faded lifetime of brutal tyranny at the hands of sin and death.

▶ **Galatians 2:20**

Indeed, I have been crucified with Christ. My ego is no longer central. It is no longer important that I appear righteous before you or have your good opinion, and I am no longer driven to impress God. Christ lives in me. The life you see me living is not "mine," but it is lived by faith in the Son of God, who loved me and gave himself for me.

▶ **Hebrews 11:6**

It's impossible to please God apart from faith. And why? Because anyone who wants to approach God must believe both that he exists and that he cares enough to respond to those who seek him.

The Adventure of Belief

TAKING A RISK ON BELIEF

In your own words, what are the benefits of risk as you embark on your adventure of belief? Consider committing one of the promises above to memory.

The following passages give a fuller picture of who you are in Christ. Do you dare to believe that what God says is true?

Memorize one of the verses below to combat your unbelief. Key truths about your identity in Christ:

I am confident in God:

> Proverbs 3:26
> Hebrews 10:19

I am victorious:

> Romans 8:37
> 2 Corinthians 2:14
> 1 John 5:4

I am free in Christ:

> Psalm 32:7
> 2 Corinthians 3:17
> John 8:36

I have the power of the Spirit:

> Acts 1:8
> Ephesians 1:19
> Ephesians 3:16

Dear God, enable me to believe what Your holy Word says about me. I believe that Jesus has come into my inner man and given me new life through the Holy Spirit. I am forgiven because of Jesus' sacrifice on the cross. I'm clean and sin has no authority over me. And I've been given a new heart. I'm a new creature in Christ. I receive Your adoption and now call You my Father. In Jesus' name, amen.

SECTION II
CHALLENGE

Challenge (chāl'ənj) *n.* A call to engage in a contest or fight. The quality of requiring full use of one's abilities, energy, and resources.

In this section, we will explore the three great challenges of a Promise Keeper: the challenges to live, to die, and to risk. These three components are essential, foundational, non-negotiable elements of the Christian faith. Without them, we wander through life in frustration. With them, life overflows with meaning, strength, and freedom.

The word "Christian" means different things to different people. To one person it means a stiff, upright, inflexible way of life, colorless and unbending. To another it means a risky, surprise-filled venture, lived tiptoe on the edge of expectation....If we get our information from the biblical material, there is no doubt that the Christian life is a dancing, leaping, daring life.

—*Eugene Peterson*

And in the end it's not the years in your life that count. It's the life in your years.

—*Abraham Lincoln*

Get busy living or get busy dying.

—*Red,* The Shawshank Redemption

I have read in Plato and Cicero sayings that are wise and very beautiful; but I have never read in either of them: "*Come unto me all ye that labor and are heavy laden.*"

—*Saint Augustine*

I have come that they may have life, and have it to the full.

—*Jesus Christ,*
John 10:10

CHAPTER 4

THE CHALLENGE TO LIVE

I GREW UP IN MODEST SURROUND-ings. Middle-class America. The Deep South. Bible-belt, churchgoing folks...and football. SEC Football. A football scholarship provided a way to college, and college football brought me new teammates, which brought me some really good friends. During my freshman year, two of those friends came to believe in Christ.

These guys were both tough characters, so their conversion and commitment to follow Jesus was a shock to the team; some doubted that it was real. But it was real: these guys were being transformed from the inside out, and they knew it. They decided that they would talk about it with anyone—anywhere and at anytime. One Sunday in church, one of them decided to get up and share what had happened to him. "I have worked my a** off for coach," he said, "and now I'm going to work my a** off for Jesus." Obviously, he had the zeal part down. The theology was still a little muddy.

Later that year, my good friend Chette Williams got a turn to share his life-changing story at a Fellowship of Christian

Athletes' meeting. He had invited a group of teammates to come and check it out (it was basically a set up). When Chette got up to "share his testimony," he turned to his group of bewildered running mates and said, "Guys, I can't go around smoking pot with you anymore. I can't stay out drinking and breaking curfew like we used to...."

He continued down the road of group confession for several miles; each step of the way, he revealed detail after detail of their nightly escapades. Naturally, his buddies were shocked. They thought this little get-together was going to be the start of a party. Bad assumption, but somehow they all survived the night. (One of them even became a pastor.) I love Chette. He's now a seminary graduate and chaplain for the Auburn University football program.

Have you been able to share your story about following Christ? If so, how did it go?

I learned a lot from those guys. Mostly, I learned that someone who has tasted the real life of God can't help but talk about it. (See Psalm 40:10.) The new life my friends had experienced was so real that it simply overflowed in their lives and in their words...colorful as those words often were. The life they had found in Jesus was something altogether better than anything they had ever known. It was richer and deeper. They were alive. It was the kind of "alive" that takes the hardest man and makes him a giver. It takes the most vulgar man and gives him a testimony to share. It takes a lost man and gives him a purpose. It gives him a life to live.

We all want to live life to the fullest and make our lives count for something. We don't want to waste our lives. We want to wake up each morning with a purpose. The problem is that somewhere along the line we got absorbed into this crazy, chaotic lifestyle that drains us of the very life we desire. Men today are often overburdened with tasks, and many are bored. Bored with their jobs. Bored with their life. At times they pay no attention to the deepest desires of their hearts—if they even know what those desires are anymore.

As followers of Christ, we have an incredible new identity. We are forgiven; we're clean. We've been adopted by the King of kings, and we have the mystery of an exchanged life going on within us. But what do we do with it? We have a hunger to experience the life God designed us to live. We can hear a distant voice saying to us, "There is more to this life than living and dying; more than trying to make it on your own." Everything in us knows we need to take a risk on God's plan—to get out of the boat and start walking toward Jesus. (See Matthew 14:29.)

Many of us would be willing to take our one shot at life and risk it all if we had an understanding of what true life is; but very few of us have found what we are looking for. As Henry David Thoreau pointed out in *Walden*, "The mass of men lead lives of quiet desperation." A life of quiet desperation is not what God intended for His sons.

FINDING LIFE

So, what is this "life"? And how could we find it if we wanted to? We don't have a lot of time for reflection in our rat race lives. Everyone is racing in every direction, turning to the right and left through a maze that seems to have no end. We move with determination—but no one knows why they are moving in the direction they're going. In their classic country song *"I'm in a Hurry and Don't Know Why,"* Alabama confesses that most of life is spent rushing around, and we don't have a clue why. In Matthew 11:28–29, Christ said, *"Come to me, all you who are weary and burdened, and I will give you rest. Take my yoke upon you and learn from me, for I am gentle and humble in heart, and you will find rest for your souls."* Let's take a break from the rat race for a moment and turn our attention to the truth of the Bible. What does it says about "life" and our desire to experience it?

Let's start off with some definitions. There are two kinds of life. The Greeks actually used two different words to describe the concept of *life*. The word *bios* refers to physical life. That's the stuff we can touch and see. (We get the English term "biology" from this word.) The other word, *Zoë*, has a much deeper meaning. Bill Ewing, in the book *Rest Assured*, describes it this way:

> *Zoë* life is what makes our biological life worth living, giving us direction, vision, and purpose. It is the search for this *Zoë* life that is the central theme in the story of all humanity. Significance, purpose, and inexpressible value are part of God's design for us.[3]

These are two different words with two entirely different concepts of "life." If we get these two ideas mixed up—and almost all of us do—we'll have huge problems as we challenge ourselves to find true life.

In our search for *Zoë* life, most of us turn to the *bios* of life. We try to find meaning, purpose, and fulfillment in material and physical things. This is the "life" most people live.

Our culture is absolutely driven by this notion. Our music promotes it. TV advertisers sell it. Our entertainment portrays it night after night. The idea is that true life can be found in what

THE CHALLENGE TO LIVE

we possess. You know how it goes: we start by thinking, "Lord, others have more than I do." We begin to question God about it: "They have better houses, God. They have cooler jobs. They get to travel. They seem to have so much more…."

I was recently watching an interview with a man on television; I don't agree with him on much, but he is extremely talented and can be very inspiring. I thought, "God, why would You give that guy so much talent and influence when he obviously doesn't give a rip about You? Here I am, trying to serve You, and I would love to have that guy's opportunities." What I was actually saying was, "God, what You provide for me isn't enough. Your purposes for me are not wise." The next day I happened to read the following passage in the book of Malachi:

> *"You have said, 'It is futile to serve God. What did we gain by carrying out his requirements and going about like mourners before the* LORD *Almighty? But now we call the arrogant blessed. Certainly the evildoers prosper, and even those who challenge God escape.'" Then those who feared the* LORD *talked with each other, and the* LORD *listened and heard. A scroll of remembrance was written in his presence concerning those who feared the* LORD *and honored his name. "They will be mine," says the* LORD *Almighty, "in the day when I make up my treasured possession. I will spare them, just as in compassion a man spares his son who serves him. And you will again see the distinction between the righteous and the wicked, between those who serve God and those who do not."* (Malachi 3:14–18)

The problem is that we often just don't believe God is good. We don't believe He delights in giving us the desires of our heart. Instead, we believe He is stingy and saves His best for others. Satan loves to feed these kinds of thoughts. As the Liar, he will always say, "God is not good. He withholds good things from you. He can't be trusted." This is essentially what Satan told Eve in the garden of Eden. (See Genesis 3:1–5.)

I obviously had to ask God to forgive me and change my understanding of His heart and Word. Not only did I not trust God's heart, but I had the biblical concepts of *Zoë* and *bios* life confused.

In your community, where do most men look for "life"?

The world is always trying to convince us that happiness and meaning in life can be found in the physical; there are a lot of rich and famous people out there who reinforce this idea. But, as you might expect, God's truth says, "*For the wisdom of this world is foolishness in God's sight. As it is written:... 'The Lord knows that the thoughts of the wise are futile'*" (1 Corinthians 3:19–20).

It's absolutely amazing, when you think about it, how driven we are by the material definition of success. We are living in one of the world's most affluent countries—when the standard of living is higher than at any other time in history—and still we feel empty and unfulfilled. It seems like we would wise up after awhile.

A DIFFERENT PATH TO LIFE

Bios has, to be certain, a certain shadowy or symbolic resemblance to Zoë, but only the sort of resemblance there is between a photo and a place, or a statue and a man. A man who is changed from having Bios to having Zoë would have gone through as big a change as a statue which was

changed from being a carved stone to being a real
man.[4]   (C. S. Lewis, *Mere Christianity*)

I think Lewis nails it here—and he speaks right to our desires.
We're ready to break out of our lives of stone and live lives as passionate, free men, but there is a deceptive detour on the road to
where we want to go.

God is calling us to something else; actually, He is calling us
to *Someone* else. In our search for true life, we must cross the lines
of conventional wisdom again; we must begin to think outside
our culture and the way the Western world has programmed our
minds. In order to find life, we must step into an area that most
theologians call "the mysterium." (That's Latin for "We really
don't have a clue what is going on.") Nonetheless, when it comes
to the search for life, the Bible points us in a very specific direction (emphases added):

> *In him was **life**, and that **life** was the light of men.*   (John 1:4)

> *I am the resurrection and the **life**. He who believes in me will live,
> even though he dies.*   (John 11:25)

> *I am the way and the truth and the **life**.*   (John 14:6)

> *When Jesus Christ, **who is your life**, appears, then you also will
> appear with him in glory.*   (Colossians 3:4)

> *He who has the Son has the **life**; he who does not have the Son of
> God does not have **life**.*   (1 John 5:12)

In these passages—and many others throughout Scripture—
Jesus Christ doesn't just say that He knows *where* life is; He
doesn't say He has some extra life lying around and He's willing
to share some of it. No, He claims that He actually *is* the life we
are searching for.

In a mysterious but very practical way, Jesus Christ *embodies* the life that we seek. Jesus Christ *is* life.

Jesus made very distinct claims about who He was, and these are directly related to His claim that He is the life that we seek.

- *He claimed to be God*: John 5:17–18, John 8:58–59, John 11:24–32

- *Others said He was God*: Isaiah 9:6, John 1:1–18, Philippians 2:6–11, Colossians 2:9–10

- *He did things that only God can do*: Matthew 9:2–7, Mark 2:5–12, John 16:29–31

- *He was described with terms and titles used only for God*: Exodus 3:14 and John 8:58; Isaiah 41:4 and Revelation 1:8; Genesis 1:14–15, Isaiah 42:5, and John 1:3; Colossians 1:16

- *He knows everything*: 1 John 3:20

- *He has all power*: Jeremiah 30 2:17, 27; Matthew 28:16–18

- *He never changes*: Malachi 3:6, Hebrews 13:8

- *He is love*: 1 John 4:8

- *He is willing to actually be our life*: 2 Corinthians 5:17–19, Galatians 2:20, Colossians 3:4

Jesus lived the perfect life. There is nothing He doesn't know; there is nothing He can't do. When He makes the claim that He is our life, He challenges us to enter into a relationship with Him—a relationship in which we see Him as the source of all life (*Zoë* life that is, not just *bios* life).

When drinking at a well on a hot and dusty day, Jesus said to a woman, "*Everyone who drinks this water will be thirsty again, but whoever drinks the water I give him will never thirst. Indeed, the water I give him will become in him a spring of water welling up to eternal life*" (John

4:13–14). Water always represents life and provision in the Bible. Jesus explained *Zoë* life to the woman at the well.

She was curious. How could this man provide life giving water? Does that mean I never have to come to back to this well? How can you never be thirsty again? *She had physical life questions that can only be answered through* Zoë *life.* Jesus was not trying to confuse her; He was giving her the right answer to the wrong question. He was putting the aspects of life in their proper order.

Zoë life flows like water. When this living water touches us, it satisfies; it refreshes; it regenerates. It brings life—not just once, but continually as we choose to stay at the well and drink. Even in the book of Revelation, the throne of God has a river of water flowing from it. (See Revelation 22:1.) That's where life is found again and again.

> **How would you explain to your unbelieving friends that "Christ is life"?**

THE WORLD IS YOURS IF YOU WANT IT

I received a small paperweight as a high school graduation gift. It said, "The World Is Yours if You Want It." Let's be honest: part of us wants the world very much. Christians and non-Christians have the same approach toward *bios* life: the non-Christian says, "I want my *own* life;" the Christian says, "God, I want You to give me the life *I* want."

We often find ourselves frustrated, disappointed, or even questioning God's character, based on what we have or don't have in our *bios* life. We want leisure. We want comfort. We want success our way. We want to be acknowledged. We want. We want. We want.

We ignore the warning in Matthew 16:26, which says, *"What good will it be for a man if he gains the whole world, yet forfeits his soul?"* We forget the wisdom of James 4:3, which says, *"When you ask, you do not receive, because you ask with wrong motives, that you may spend what you get on your pleasures."*

As parents, we try to help our children get a better perspective on thankfulness when they are constantly asking for more. Recently, I was driving home from church with my four-year-old in the back seat. Out of the blue, he asked me for one hundred dollars. He is still learning to count to twenty, so one hundred dollars has no context. *This is a great opportunity to give him a little Kingdom lesson*, I thought. "Christian, everything I have is yours," I said. "You are my son. And everything I own is yours." He immediately asked, "Is it worth one hundred dollars?"

Much of our frustration in our *bios* life is because we lack a proper perspective. We do not see the value and worth of our salvation or the richness and generosity of our God. God has been generous with us beyond comparison. He has given us everything. We are His sons, and we will inherit His Kingdom. Through His grace, we have eternal life, peace, joy, forgiveness, and fellowship. He has given us His Son, lives in us, and is the source of the life we seek.

So what kind of life do we ask God for? Our desires are revealed by our prayers. If we want God to change our *bios* life—to change others to meet our needs, or to give us the physical things we want—then we keep asking and asking and asking, expecting that the world should be ours. And sometimes God gives us what we ask for to teach us about real life.

I have always loved attention. Even when I was a kid, an opportunity to get some stage time was everything. As my dad might say, "This is sad but true." I might have seemed relaxed in a crowd of people, but on the inside my heart was always saying, "Somebody just give me a microphone!" I always felt that I had so much to say, so much I could "give" (a code word for "get more attention")...if only I had the chance.

I got my chance on a night I'll never forget.

Years ago, I was helping stage a Christian concert after a minor league baseball game. There were about four thousand people in the stands that night, and when the game was finished, we were ready to go. I stood up to give the band a quick intro when *zap!*—the band's PA system broke down. The guys in the band looked at me and said, "Stretch the introduction! It's going to take us about thirty minutes to fix this problem."

Thirty minutes to fix the problem. Man, that's a lifetime with one microphone and four thousand people. But wait a minute, isn't this just what I've always wanted? This is my big shot! It's me and everybody else, and I'm in the spotlight!

I quickly reached into the vast amounts of material that I had been storing in my mind for such an opportunity: all the witty, profound things that I had been waiting to share. It lasted about four minutes and thirteen seconds. I timed it. Twenty-six minutes to go...and I was out of juice.

I decided to do a sing-along. (Brilliant idea.) My dad had been a US Marine, so I started with the Marine Corps hymn. On a scale of 1 to 10, I'd say it came off about 2.3. Then somebody yelled, "Let's sing the Air Force hymn!" I knew it said something about the "wild blue yonder," and that's where I started. The desecration lasted three minutes and nine seconds. After a total of sixteen minutes and forty-three seconds, I had successfully offended every single man and woman in the United States armed forces.

So I started telling jokes. (Another brilliant idea.) I'm not all that funny to begin with, and telling jokes is an art. It took me another nine minutes to realize that there is a huge difference between a friend laughing *with* you and a stadium of thousands of people laughing *at* you. In the stands, I could see horror in my wife Jenny's eyes. She kept shaking her head and desperately looking at me like, "Please, please, don't continue." Many in the crowd began to head for the exits.

This was my heart's desire only days before. Now, all I wanted was some sort of escape hatch, something to make me invisible, or maybe just a cyanide capsule. I felt like God was saying, "You got anything else you want to say, Burkhalter?"

I dropped the microphone on the pitcher's mound and walked off. When I got to the dugout, my buddies were falling all over themselves in laughter. "So Todd, why *did* the chicken cross the road?!" they hooted between their tears.

Yeah, that was my big opportunity in the spotlight. The only problem in asking God for selfish things is that sometimes He lets us have them to remind us that the world has no *Zoë* life to offer.

THE CHALLENGE TO LIVE

Perhaps the most tragic reality of all is that most men will reach the end of their lives with a haunting realization that they've missed it—their one shot at making life count. They will turn around at the end and see that the road they were on did not take them where they had hoped. They will know that decades have slipped away behind them, and the years were wasted on things that had the appearance of life but not the substance of life that is found only in Jesus Christ.

That, in my opinion, is the ultimate tragedy: a wasted life. Many guys have a "good" life and don't realize that their potential is being spent on things that don't really matter at all. It doesn't have to be that way. God has made the way to life clear; now He places the challenge to live before us.

We are being called to a life where the Spirit of Christ will overflow into our *bios* (or physical) lives. Again, this is the exact opposite of what the world expects. While others believe that physical existence should overflow into the spiritual life, the Bible has made it clear that this is not the case. Remarkable things begin to happen when life is lived the other way around, focusing on our relationship with Jesus Christ as the source of life:

Perspective. We begin to see things as they truly are. No longer fooled by the illusions of the world, we can see the lies of materialism for what they are and begin to focus our passions toward Christ.

Purpose. By understanding that Christ is our life, we can face each day with a new sense of direction. We finally know where life is to be found, and we can see the opportunities to share the truth with those around us.

Power. When we begin to really believe the truth that Jesus is God, we can begin to live in a way that is consistent with who He is. That unleashes the strength and power of His resurrection in our lives. The power of the resurrection sets everything in order.

Passion. Devotion is fleeting in the world; the things of *bios* cannot give us truth or life. As life begins to fall under the perspective, purpose, and power of Jesus Christ, however, a growing sense of godly passion emerges in our souls. Feelings may come and go, but, deep inside, a heartfelt commitment to God emerges in our relationship with Him through Jesus Christ.

This is the great challenge to live and find our meaning, purpose, and direction in our relationship with Jesus. When we do that, His life naturally begins to flow through us in powerful ways that spread out into the physical realm around us. When we find life in Christ, we not only find the love that we deeply desire, but His love becomes unleashed through us—it flows supernaturally from the inside out.

When it comes to "life," the choice is yours. You can choose the physical or you can choose Christ. That is the ongoing decision in the challenge to live.

RISK ASSESSMENT

▶ Each person is only granted one life. How does that affect your willingness to take risks?

▶ In your quest for life, what are the consequences of choosing poorly? What would it be like to reach the end of life, look back, and realize that you had made the wrong choices?

▶ If you were to begin seeking Christ first and devoting your life to His kingdom, how might that change your physical life? Could it be a threat to your existing lifestyle and beliefs?

▶ Take an honest inventory of your own life. Where are you in your search for life? What are you not willing to risk?

THE REWARDS OF RISK

▶ **Matthew 6:33**

Steep your life in God-reality, God-initiative, God-provisions. Don't worry about missing out. You'll find all your everyday human concerns will be met.

▶ **Matthew 8:22**

Jesus refused. "First things first. Your business is life, not death. Follow me. Pursue life."

▶ **1 Peter 1:17–19**

You call out to God for help and he helps—he's a good Father that way. But don't forget, he's also a responsible Father, and won't let you get by with sloppy living. Your life is a journey you must travel with a deep consciousness of God. It cost God plenty to get you out of that dead-end, empty-headed life you grew up in. He paid with Christ's sacred blood, you know.

TAKING A RISK ON LIFE

With a pen and a blank piece of paper, take your Bible to a place where you can be alone for awhile. Spend some time praying and talking to God about all you've learned so far; then open your Bible and spend a little time thinking about Philippians 3:8. In *The Message* Bible, this verse says:

THE CHALLENGE TO LIVE

Yes, all the things I once thought were so important are gone from my life. Compared to the high privilege of knowing Christ Jesus as my Master, firsthand, everything I once thought I had going for me is insignificant—dog dung. I've dumped it all in the trash so that I could embrace Christ and be embraced by him.

On the paper, make a list of the most important things in your life right now; then list the things you want out of life in the future. Here comes the symbolic risk: at the top of the list, write out Philippians 3:8. You are making a statement that says, "Compared to Christ, I consider these things to be insignificant. Jesus is my life; these things are not." Then crumple up the list and, with a prayer of dedication, throw it in the trash.

Dear Father God, I acknowledge that Jesus Christ is the beginning and the end. I believe that all things were made by Him, for Him, and through Him. Teach me more about Your Son Jesus so that I might have perspective, purpose, power, and passion for life. In Jesus' name, amen.

He is no fool who gives up what he cannot keep to gain what he cannot lose.

—*Jim Elliot*

Every man dies, not every man really lives.

—*William Wallace,* Braveheart

My religious belief teaches me to feel as safe in battle as in bed. God has fixed the time for my death, I do not concern myself with that. But to be always ready whenever it my overtake me. That is the way all men should live and all men would be equally brave.

—*Stonewall Jackson,* Gods and Generals

Master Yoda, you can't die.   —*Luke Skywalker*

Strong am I with the Force, but not that strong.   —*Yoda*

I tell you the truth, unless a kernel of wheat falls to the ground and dies, it remains only a single seed. But if it dies, it produces many seeds. The man who loves his life will lose it, while the man who hates his life in this world will keep it for eternal life.

—*Jesus Christ,*
John 12:24–25

CHAPTER 5

I GREW UP IN THE SMALL TOWN of Leeds, Alabama. Not necessarily the capital of commerce and trade for the great state of Alabama. Not the cultural center of the Southeast, either. However, we did have our own Arts Council that put on small plays in the summer. And we did have a Leeds girl who was the runner-up to Miss America when I was a teenager. That was a big deal.

But our little city was known for something more. In a town that only had a Pizza Hut and a Dairy Queen to serve our evening cuisine, we had three Congressional Medal of Honor recipients. This medal is the highest distinction given by the United States to any individual. Most recipients have received it in death. They often died during the extraordinary acts of bravery for which the medal is awarded. In the history of the United States, just over 3,400 men and women have received this honor…and our little town had three of them.

Because of this, Leeds became known as the "City of Valor"—a place where heroes live. Mr. Erwin lived just two houses from mine. In 1945, he carried a burning phosphate bomb through the fuselage of a B-29 with his bare hands while crawling on his belly. With the plane completely engulfed in smoke, he threw the bomb from the damaged aircraft, saving the lives of the entire crew.

As I was growing up, I would see Mr. Erwin from time to time, noticing the scars on his hands and the disfigured flesh on his face. I remember him as a patriot and a man of great courage. Nearly every culture on earth lifts up those who are willing to sacrifice themselves for the greater good. We look up to men and women who make great sacrifices at great personal expense— particularly those who were willing to risk their lives for others.

The movie *Glory* captures the heart of valor powerfully as well. It's the historic tale of the Massachusetts 54th Regiment in the Civil War—the first regiment of African-American soldiers. The movie reveals the hardships and barriers that these men faced just to reach the battlefield. The night before their attack on Fort Wagner, in the face of overwhelming odds and almost certain death, a soldier shares these words around the campfire as a last living testament:

> If tomorrow is our great gettin' up morning, if tomorrow we have to meet the judgment day, Heavenly Father, we want You to let our folks know that we died facing the enemy, we want them to know that we went down standing up, amongst those that are fightin' against our oppression, we want them to know, Heavenly Father, that we died for freedom.[5]

Words like that resonate in the heart of every man. There's something in us that wants to risk it all for something greater than our own selfish concerns. Deep inside we desire to die for a purpose worthy of the "last full measure of our devotion," as Abraham Lincoln said during the Gettysburg Address.

A DIFFERENT KIND OF SACRIFICE

It's natural to take our worldly understanding of valor and inject it into our spiritual lives. There's a natural instinct to want to sacrifice for God. I don't want to be misunderstood at this point; I believe Christians have a calling to live lives of sacrifice. *But*...unless we are building our lives on foundational biblical truths, our attempts at self-sacrifice—even for the cause of Christ—will miss the mark.

Who are your heroes? What qualities make them stand out in your mind?

Earthy sacrifice is not the key to salvation. (See Hosea 6:6; Isaiah 1:11–18, 66:1–3.) Certainly, each of us as Christian men faces the challenge to die to self. It is crucial that we have a solid understanding of how we are to do that. If not, we are going to miss the point of the gospel of God's grace altogether.

Let's consider for a moment the history, values, and vision of Promise Keepers. In 1990, Coach Bill McCartney found that *Webster's Dictionary* described the word *integrity* with synonyms such as "candor, truthfulness, honesty, honor, and uprightness" and with the descriptive phrase "one who keeps promises." Consequently, he named the emerging organization "Promise Keepers." The ministry's slogan under its new name became "Men of Integrity." Christlike integrity and its inherent character are the foundation of Promise Keepers and the core of its message.

A Promise Keeper is committed...

1. To honoring Jesus Christ through worship, prayer, and obedience to God's Word in the power of the Holy Spirit.

2. To pursuing vital relationships with a few other men, understanding that he needs brothers to help him keep his promises.

3. To practicing spiritual, moral, ethical, and sexual purity.

4. To building strong marriages and families through love, protection, and biblical values.

5. To supporting the mission of his church by honoring and praying for his pastor and by actively giving his time and resources.

6. To reaching beyond any racial and denominational barriers to demonstrate the power of biblical unity.

7. To influencing his world, being obedient to the Great Commandment (see Mark 12:30–31) and the Great Commission (see Matthew 28:19–20).

That's a very tall order. To fulfill such commitments requires *more* strength than any man possesses in himself; the man who attempts to accomplish such things in his own power faces certain defeat.

The life of a man who seeks to offer his best for God in his own strength resembles the proverbial roller-coaster ride. The roller coaster heads up the tracks, pushed on by the inspiration of a good book, a conference, a worship song, or even the conviction that his life should be different. Normally, a man sets before himself rules and guidelines to follow for God. He wants to free himself from a particular sin or temptation, love his wife more, be more patient with his children, or serve as the spiritual leader of his home; all these are noble aspirations, of course, and perhaps he can do these things in his own strength…for awhile. But Gordon England explains the frustration men feel when they try to sacrifice themselves and change their act:

> It's like a carpenter trying to do brain surgery. He can open the skull, but it gets messy in a hurry. What's broken is not our behavior. Our behavior only demonstrates that we are living in a broken relationship with our heavenly Father.[6]

THE ONLY SACRIFICE THAT MATTERS

I'm going to cross a line here. I want to step beyond what our reason and physical reality say is possible.

Maybe it's time to consider something contrary to our normal experience. If the way we've been doing things hasn't been working, maybe it's time to consider something so "out there" that it just might work….What I'm suggesting is this: *the reason that many men have difficulty living the Christian life is that they don't realize that they have already died.* I'm going to back this idea up with God's Word and let it speak for itself:

> *I have been crucified with Christ and I no longer live, but Christ lives in me. The life I live in the body, I live by faith in the Son of God, who loved me and gave himself for me.* (Galatians 2:20)

I don't claim to understand how this works. It's supernatural. But God's Word says it over and over again. Everything about us is affected by Christ's death and resurrection. In God's eyes, I was crucified when Christ was crucified. When I turned my life over to Him, His death became mine…and His resurrection also became mine. The power that raised Him from the dead is also at work in me.

In a sense, I don't live anymore; Christ lives in me. Sure, my body might look the same, my thoughts might seem the same, and my feelings might feel the same; but inside, there has been a transformation…and it's a radical one.

In true biblical conversion and regeneration of a man's soul, there must be a revolution: death to the old structures of living and managing life without Christ to following Christ as Lord and Leader. When a man surrenders his life to the Lordship of Jesus Christ, a spiritual transaction takes place within him. Christ invades, confronts, and overthrows the dark, self-centered seats of power in the human soul. The spirit of life in Christ has replaced the spirit of sin and death. The man we used to be actually died and has been replaced by the new man that God is making us into. We had to die so that the life of Christ could be revealed in us. Now this great mystery has become our life: "*I no longer live, but Christ lives in me*" (Galatians 2:20).

Augustine, the great theologian and early church father, faced a similar situation. He had lived a "carefree life" before becoming a Christian. As he passed by a former mistress, the young woman began calling to him, "Augustine, Augustine, it is I." Augustine turned and said kindly, "Yes, but it is no longer I." A death had occurred. Augustine had died. The man he once was had experienced a rebirth. The new man was emerging.

Here comes the ultimate course correction. *We are often told that we need to "die to self." But the challenge is not really to die, but to see ourselves as already having died and now experiencing new life through Christ.* The implications of this are astounding because we were crucified with Christ; Scripture says we are already dead to many things:

We are dead to sin. Our bodies and minds are still vulnerable to temptation, but in the core of our being—on the level of our true identity—we're dead to sin now.

> *If we have been united with him like this in his death, we will certainly also be united with him in his resurrection. For we know that our old self was crucified with him so that the body of sin might be done away with, that we should no longer be slaves to sin—because anyone who has died has been freed from sin.*
>
> (Romans 6:5–7)

We are dead to legalism. In general, men feel the need to work to earn salvation and acceptance before God and other men. The Bible says that the rules of the law have no effect on us anymore. We are recreated to focus on our relationship with Christ and not on the rule of law. However, our relationship with Christ will never lead us to violate the moral law of God.

> *So, my brothers, you also died to the law through the body of Christ, that you might belong to another, to him who was raised from the dead, in order that we might bear fruit to God.* (Romans 7:4)

We are dead to the way the world works. Let's face it: the world judges us continually based on our performance. Because we've been crucified with Christ, the expectations of the world need not control us anymore. There is a new freedom to listen to Jesus Christ and to follow Him boldly if—and only if—we have died to such petty rules and instructions and

What religious expectations have you tried to live up to in order to please others?

moved on to something far more powerful and profound: a vital relationship with the living Christ.

If you have died with Christ to the elementary principles of the world, why, as if you were living in the world, do you submit yourself to decrees, such as, "Do not handle, do not taste, do not touch!" (Colossians 2:20–21 NASB)

In what ways do you see Christian men trying to become something that God says they already are in Christ?

This is extreme stuff; it is contrary to conventional wisdom. All these things came about because of Jesus Christ's ability to keep all of God's laws perfectly. None of our efforts were needed. God accomplished all these things in *His* own strength. We don't have to try to make something happen or offer God a sacrifice for something He has already done through His Son. This is good news. Actually, you'll never get better news. But unfortunately, men are still driven almost to the brink of insanity as they try to become something that they already are!

The power of this revolutionary truth is unleashed in our lives when we choose to act according to what Scripture says is true about us. This is one of the great adventures for truth; it is an opportunity to align our lives with what God says—to take Him at His word and see what happens! By discovering what is true about us in Christ, we can experience an entirely different outlook on life. We can respond to things around us in a way that is consistent with God's transforming presence in our lives. No more formulas. No more lists of behaviors to modify or accentuate our own strength. No more keeping score of the sins of others and reporting back on the results. Christ alone. Jesus Christ in us.

THE CHALLENGE TO DIE

OUR LIVES BELONG TO GOD

In Christianity, there is a popular and noble-sounding ambition that many men strive for: *to die to self*. This can mean a lot of things to a lot of different people, but normally *dying to self* means that someone tries to do his very best in order to say "no" to his own desires.

If we have been crucified and raised with Christ, He now lives in us, and our lives belong to Him. What we really need to die to is the notion that our lives belong to us. Our lives are not our own. They are not ours to lay down for someone else because we don't own them. Our lives belong to God.

The challenge to die is to understand that our old nature dies when we accept Christ, and we are filled with His new life by His Holy Spirit. Now we live according to His promises and the declaration of who He says we are in Him.

Should He desire us to live, we live.

Should He desire us to wait, we wait.

Should He desire us to go, then we go.

Should He desire us to die, then we die.

Like the African-American soldiers from the 54th Massachusetts who attacked Fort Wagner during those critical days of the Civil War, we too are men under orders. And like soldiers, we go to the battle knowing that *"to me, to live is Christ and to die is gain"* (Philippians 1:21). Our lives are no longer our own. They have been signed over to God the Father in blood—the blood of Jesus Christ, the perfect and final sacrifice.

Your old life is dead. Your new life, which is your real life—even though invisible to spectators—is with Christ in God. He is your life.　　　　　　　　　　(Colossians 3:3 MSG)

WE LIVE BY FAITH

It takes faith to follow the Lord and give Him complete control. This kind of faith can move mountains, allowing us to overcome things that we have struggled with our whole lives. We simply submit and accept, trusting in what we know to be true about His character and what He says about us, regardless of what we see.

When I first began taking flight lessons, I learned to fly VFR (Visual Flight Rules). That means you can only fly when you have a certain amount of visibility. Most pilots try to complete their IFR (Instrument Flight Rules) as well. This trains you to fly using only the instruments—without looking outside at all. You are discouraged from relying on your instincts or senses. In this training, you wear a helmet with a completely black face shield that allows you to see only the instruments. You learn to rely on the instruments for everything related to course headings. You're told countless stories of pilot error where a fatal crash occurred because the pilot didn't trust his instruments.

God has given us the instrument of His Word. He warns us to live by it and not by what we can see humanly or by how we feel emotionally. His Word is always giving us course corrections. We need these because God knows that our natural instincts are flawed and our own abilities to navigate are useless. (See Jeremiah 10:23.)

God has His own design for success, *and it is not dependent on our own effort, strength, or sacrifice.* (See Isaiah 66:3–4.) What He desires is a relationship through the sacrifice that has been made in the life, death, and resurrection of Jesus Christ. Jesus is the key to the relationship that God desires with us. We are able to live in a vital relationship with God only through *His* sacrifice.

THE CHALLENGE TO DIE

God doesn't desire our self-directed *performance*; He desires a Christ-directed *relationship*. Therefore, the Christian life is not designed to be self-directed or self-empowered but to be lived in the power of Christ's infinite strength. The co-founder and CEO of Integrity Music, Mike Coleman, takes a faith-based approach to business. "Our company's mission statement is 'Helping people worldwide experience the manifest presence of God,'" he says. "That is impossible for us to do on our own. We are absolutely dependent on God's strength and provisions to complete the work we've been called to...and that's not a bad place to be."

We are to pursue a relationship with God where personal connection is the goal and strong action is the result. Putting faith to work is one of the great adventures of the Christian life; it's your opportunity to take your one shot at life and make it count for the kingdom of God.

WHEN FAITH COMES HOME

My mother and I have always been the best of friends. When she was diagnosed with cancer, we decided we would believe in God to do the miraculous. The doctors had a bleak outlook on what was going to happen, but Mom and I would just smile at each other when they brought us bad news or when they told us the end might be near. We knew that God was able to do *"what is impossible with men"* (Luke 18:27). And so we continued to believe and pray that she would be made well. We agreed to hold firmly to faith, even if it made us look foolish to those around us. We committed to saying to one another, "We believe God is able to heal our bodies. We believe

What are the most difficult things for you to entrust to God? Why do you think these are so hard?

that He will heal us...." That was our prayer; our statement of faith. Regardless of how foolish we may have looked to others, we were going to believe in faith that God would heal my mom.

He didn't. In January 2006, my mom died. And it was a heartache beyond what I thought was possible. I mean, it was a fall-down-on-the-ground heartache. It wasn't just grief; it was anger and frustration with God. In the midst of my own questioning, in the midst of my complaining and anger, God interrupted. He interrupted me like a father would interrupt a crying child who's exhausted. He didn't interrupt me with a spanking; He interrupted me with an embrace. And in that embrace, God gently gave me a thought to consider:

My mother's death was like a calculus problem.

I can still work a few math problems on a chalkboard. Math has just always made sense to me. I understand how it works. I know how to get from the initial problem to the solution. If my five-year-old son, however, wanted to learn calculus, there would be a problem. The problem would not be in my inability to actually solve the problems or my lack of ability to teach the math; it would be in his inability to understand it. It just wouldn't make sense to him.

Your mother's death is like a calculus problem, God showed me as He embraced my weary heart. *Life and death are like an equation that you can't understand, but it makes perfect sense to Me; I understand the math. It's not the fact that I can't explain it to you, Todd, or the fact that I can't solve the problem. The problem is that you can't understand it. You're a five-year-old trying to understand calculus. Trust Me that you're seeing dimly through a mirror. There will be a day when you see it all clearly. You'll see this problem on the board as it relates to the way your mother lived and died, and it'll make perfect sense to you...but not today.*

The Challenge to Die

At that moment, I faced the challenge to die. I had a choice to make: Would I place my faith in God as I knew Him to be from Scripture? Or would I judge Him because of the way I perceived Him to be dealing with my problem? I chose to be the five-year-old in the embrace of an all-knowing, loving Father. There are still days when I feel overwhelmed with sadness, but I don't labor against it any longer. I've come to rest in the fact that God knows the math. And I do not. But one day I will.

God owns all that there is, including me (and my mom). He does as He wills. He is God and we are not. I had a mentor who would always say, "God is just. He doesn't need me to justify Him." It is our job to trust His heart, even when things He allows or causes are hard or painful to accept.

A LIVING DEATH

There is a flip side to this coin. Recognizing that we have been crucified with Christ must lead us to the conclusion that God owns our lives and that we are to live by faith in Him. But *dying to self* means we recognize not only that we are dead, but also that we are alive in Christ.

When we see ourselves as crucified with Christ—recognizing that Christ now lives in us—then we find the key to living a victorious Christian life. It is through this lens that we can see the things that He can do through us. Our role is to submit ourselves to God and allow Him to complete His work, using us in any way He sees fit. Why would God ask us to consider committing to the seven promises of a Promise Keeper? Is it because He has confidence in our efforts? No! It's because He has confidence in *Himself*. His Spirit working through our lives can accomplish things that would be impossible for us to do on our own. God is alive in us. We simply need to acknowledge His sovereignty and rulership over all things in life and pray, *"Not my will, but yours be done"* (Luke 22:42). Consider these words of Jesus:

> *I am the vine; you are the branches. If a man remains in me and I in him, he will bear much fruit; apart from me you can do nothing.*
>
> (John 15:5)

These are emphatic words. He doesn't say that there are *some* things we can do; He says there is *nothing* we can do on our own. On the outside, it might look as if we are accomplishing great things for God and His kingdom. But if it's not His life living through us, then it accomplishes nothing of lasting value. When we allow Him to do it, though, the possibilities are unlimited:

> *I can do everything through him who gives me strength.*
>
> (Philippians 4:13)

> *I tell you the truth, anyone who has faith in me will do what I have been doing. He will do even greater things than these, because I am going to the Father.*
>
> (John 14:12)

The challenge to die does not depend on our strength or our desire to do what God calls us to do. The challenge to die is to see ourselves as already dead and simply to allow God to live His life through us. When faced with temptation, opportunity, or challenge, we are to respond, "I can't, but You can, Lord Jesus."

In a relationship with the loving Lord, we will find this type of obedience to be anything but a sacrifice. Sure, there will be regular struggles with the desires of our bodies, the temptations of the world, and the lies of the devil that bombard us; but over time, the indwelling presence of Christ will work to destroy all associations within a man to the old monarchy of self-centeredness and darkness. It's the only way out of the pit of pride, ego, and self-absorption.

This is the great exchange: your life for His life in you. It gives us something entirely different to focus our lives on. You're dead. Your life is no longer your life. True life is found in living out that death, relying only on the life of Christ in you.

You don't have to crucify yourself. It's already been done. In Colossians 3:1–3, Paul described the crucified and resurrected life:

> *Since, then, you have been raised with Christ, set your hearts on things above, where Christ is seated at the right hand of God. Set your minds on things above, not on earthly things. For you died, and your life is now hidden with Christ in God.*

God may or may not pave the way for great acts of sacrifice in your future. Should they come, they will not be of your choosing. God might work through you in ways that bring you great recognition and honor in the eyes of men. Perhaps He will use you for simple acts of service that only He sees. So be it. Just remember that it's not your life; it's His.

Christ's indwelling power can withstand intense temptations; He might choose you to reach an entire nation of people with the gospel; Christ, in you, can become a great dad to your children and a faithful husband to your wife. People might even praise you for what they see happening through your life. But you'll just smile and reflect on the truth: it wasn't you; it was Him, and you just had the best seat in the house to watch Him work—through you.

Heck, you might even receive the Congressional Medal of Honor—in which case you would feel right at home in Leeds, Alabama.

RISK ASSESSMENT

▶ How does our performance-based culture influence your efforts to please God? What sacrifices are you still trying to make to earn His acceptance?

▶ How have you handled disappointment when God didn't answer your prayers the way you wished?

▶ Do you still feel like it's *your* life, or do you see yourself as owned by God?

THE REWARDS OF RISK

► **Romans 7:5**

For as long as we lived that old way of life, doing whatever we felt we could get away with, sin was calling most of the shots as the old law code hemmed us in. And this made us all the more rebellious. In the end, all we had to show for it was miscarriages and stillbirths.

► **Romans 6:7–9**

What we believe is this: If we get included in Christ's sin-conquering death, we also get included in his life-saving resurrection. We know that when Jesus was raised from the dead it was a signal of the end of death-as-the-end. Never again will death have the last word.

► **2 Corinthians 12:9**

And then he told me, "My grace is enough; it's all you need. My strength comes into its own in your weakness." Once I heard that, I was glad to let it happen. I quit focusing on the handicap and began appreciating the gift. It was a case of Christ's strength moving in on my weakness.

RISKING IT ALL TO DIE

Certificate of Death

Year of death: 33 AD

Current date:

Cause of death: Crucifixion

Details of the deceased: As a child of the most high God and a follower of His truth as revealed in the Bible, I hereby declare my own death. According to the truth of Scripture, I recognize that I was crucified with Christ, and I no longer live. As a dead man, I have nothing to offer the kingdom of God. As a dead man, my life has already been taken from me. I have nothing left to sacrifice and nothing left to offer of myself.

I fully embrace the possibilities of this reality. My life is now His life, and He can do with it as He chooses. Through His strength I can do all things; without Him, I can do nothing.

I hereby recognize an entirely new way of living. I recognize His ownership of all things. I choose to live by faith in who He says I am. By His grace, I will choose to no longer depend on my own strength and in my own efforts of self-sacrifice. I will no longer believe that I am accepted based on my performance.

Date of authorization:

Signature of the deceased:

Lord Jesus Christ, remove any barriers that would hinder me from believing that I have been crucified with Christ. Reinforce in me that the life I once lived is gone, and that I now live by faith in Jesus Christ my Savior. I no longer need to offer any sacrifice other than my belief. The price is paid for my past, present, and future sins. Thank You for Your mercy. In Jesus' holy name, amen.

Only those who dare to fail greatly can ever achieve greatly.

—*Robert F. Kennedy*

Security is mostly a superstition. It does not exist in nature, nor do the children of men as a whole experience it. Avoiding danger is no safer in the long run than outright exposure. Life is either a daring adventure or nothing.

—*Helen Keller*

I am always doing that which I cannot do, in order that I may learn how to do it.

—*Pablo Picasso*

From now on, we live in a world where man has walked on the moon. And it's not a miracle, we just decided to go.

—*Jim Lovell,* APOLLO 13

You come to a point in your life when you really don't care what people think about you, you just care what you think about yourself.

—*Evel Knievel*

We can boldly quote, "God is there, ready to help; I'm fearless no matter what. Who or what can get to me?"

—*Hebrews 13:6* (MSG)

CHAPTER 6

WHEN I WAS A BOY, I WANTED to be evil. Not evil as in "bad," but evil as in Evel Knievel.

He jumped over stuff: buses, fountains, and long lines of cars. He was the coolest; he was the ultimate risk taker. He also looked the part. Evel Knievel had this incredible white jumpsuit with blue stars that crossed over his chest...and a collar that stood up a little bit like Elvis's. Not a lot of guys could pull off the white jumpsuit, but Evel Knievel did it. He also had some poofy-haired blonde girls in white jumpsuits with blue stars and flipped up collars that followed him everywhere he went. (That didn't mean much to me when I was eight, but when I was fourteen, it dawned on me that he had a pretty good thing going on.)

As kids, we built many a ramp around my house in honor of the great Knievel. About the time he jumped his Harley-Davidson over thirteen buses in the Houston Astrodome, I started jumping my bike over the curb. The year that he attempted his greatest jump of all—strapping himself into a rocket-powered motorcycle that propelled him over the depths of Snake River Canyon—I

117

made my greatest jump as well: over my mom and dad's picnic table. The bike was completely destroyed when I reentered the atmosphere. Actually, the bike belonged to my friend's older brother. He almost killed us after that, but that's not the point, really.

The point is this: We were designed for risk. Boys know this in their hearts, but most men have forgotten. The organic heart of a man is still represented in that boy's heart. We know it's true. We want to risk. But have we forgotten how?

THE MISSING RISK FACTOR

Maybe it started in junior high. Somewhere between the playground and the hallways, we realized that it's not smart to risk. It's better to protect ourselves and be different people in a world that might attack who we really are.

Maybe it continued in high school and college when we learned that there was a different set of rules to live by. For the first ten years, they taught us to walk and to talk. For the next ten years, they told us to sit down and be quiet. Many of us did. In the process, we learned that it was dangerous to dream outside of the box or to speak our minds.

After we entered the "real" world as adults, we were told it was time to settle down, be productive, and get a "real" job. We entered this phase of life with great expectations, but many of us lost our way and were swept away in the river of a culture going nowhere. When we got there, many of us felt lost and disoriented. We thought of trying a different road, but changing course was risky too. "Better to be safe," we were told. "Keep your health insurance current. Protect your retirement. Stay on the proven path."

The Challenge to Risk it All

What has stolen our willingness to risk it all? Fear? Yes, but not real fear—not the fear that is stimulated by a natural threat and fills our veins with adrenaline, preparing us for battle or defense. No, the thief is *false* fear—fear that erects a frightening barrier between us and the risk that we so desperately need to feel alive and act in faith.

You've undoubtedly become all too familiar with a few of these fears. You know what they sound like in your mind:

The fear of failure: "What if I try and don't succeed? I don't think I can handle another failure. I can't risk losing everything!"

The fear of rejection: "What if I give it my all and my all isn't good enough? I could be humiliated, criticized, or—worse yet—considered a failure by my friends and family."

The fear of being real: "What if I risk it all in relationships? I could share my feelings and come off looking like a fool. I could be taken advantage of; I could be exposed."

The fear of death: "What if this costs me my physical life?" We spend the vast majority of our lives trying to protect and preserve our lives. We take our vitamins and watch our cholesterol to try to avoid the inevitable, but, tragically, the false fear of death steals the very life we are afraid of losing.

We need risk, but, because of fear, "responsible" men learn to reduce risk through a variety of mechanisms—some biblical and some not. Entire industries can give us "risk assessments" for our homes, our vehicles, and our investments. To some extent, we have an internal risk assessment constantly going on. We continually balance the risk and the rewards, the cost and the payoff.

Assess the risk. Minimize the risk. We do this in our spiritual lives, too. We've learned to protect our hearts and limit our dreams. For too many of us, Christianity means little more than sitting in something called a "pew." We play along and go through the motions, but inside we wonder if this is all there is.

In your opinion, what are the main fears men wrestle with in today's world? How do these fears keep men from being risk-takers?

In our Western culture, what real risks do we take in our Christian lives? When you think about it, not all that much. Our faith has been bound up by our fear. We have been imprisoned by our anxieties. Our lives have been stolen away by false concerns. We've lost an essential component of our manhood. We should be legitimately concerned that fear has crippled us, neutralized us, and scared us into lives that are irrelevant, impotent, and ineffective in this world—and in eternity.

Fear is not the opposite of faith. Fear is the opposite of love. That's an important distinction to make. Fear comes from a lack of practical belief in an ever-present, loving God.

The Bible says that *"there is no fear in love,"* and that *"perfect love drives out fear"* (1 John 4:18). The more we embrace the love of Father God, the more fear evaporates in the light of His presence. Our fears simply cannot stand up to the presence of God. The power of believing that God really loves us, and that He is truly present in us, sets us free from our fears. In 2 Timothy, Paul confidently stated, *"For God has not given us a spirit of fear, but of power and of love and of a sound mind"* (2 Timothy 1:7 NKJV).

It's time to rediscover the adventure of risking it all.

The Challenge to Risk it All

RISK RECOVERED

I've always liked the name Caleb. We tend to name our children after these kinds of men: men of courage, men who would take a risk, men who would believe...men like Joshua, David, Paul, and Timothy. I can't remember any boys in our church's Sunday school program named Judas, Herod, Nero, or Ahab. It just doesn't happen. But men of vision who were willing to risk it all still have their names on Sunday school roles thousands of years later. Much of what attracts us to these men is what we long to see in our own lives. These were men who believed God and acted.

Caleb, in my opinion, is in rare air—an extraordinary man in the Scriptures, and an original risk-taker. He was part of a group of twelve guys that were sent out by Moses to survey or spy out the Promised Land. (See Numbers 13–14.) God had already given the Israelites ownership of the land; it was already deeded to them from God with a promise to Abraham through Moses. Ownership of the land was never in question. They were sent out as surveyors to plot the rivers, valleys, pastures, vegetation, and the people who would have to be "removed" as the nation of Israel took possession of the land and of the promise.

The question was simple: "What's it gonna take to get in there, and where do we want to live?" When they returned, the reports of the other surveyors were concerning. Ten of the twelve guys basically said, "It's very appealing, but it could put us in a situation where somebody might get hurt. We checked with our lawyers, and they said that we could be held liable for such injuries, opening ourselves up to a possible class-action lawsuit. And by the way, who started calling this the 'Promised Land' in the first place?" God had.

God had sworn an oath on Himself concerning the land. He swore on Himself because there was no one greater to swear upon. When God makes a promise, it's a done deal. But in spite of God's promise, the people responded in fear. The scouts said, in effect, "There are giants in this land. The place is fortified beyond belief. Compared to these guys, we look like grasshoppers." (See Numbers 13:27–33.)

Caleb and Joshua had a different perspective. They said, "*We'll have them for lunch! They have no protection and God is on our side. Don't be afraid of them!*" (Numbers 14:9 MSG). Not only did it look like an open house, but dinner was being served. Milk and honey were on the menu, and Caleb and Joshua were the only ones ready to make the move.

Twelve men. Each was a respected leader in his tribe. Each saw similar things. But Caleb and Joshua saw things from a different perspective. Their confidence was not based on their ability to manage the risk of facing the Giants. It was founded in what God had already spoken. They had the same information as their teammates, and yet God's promise was enough to propel them to believe—and then propel them to act.

So, ten men came back with a thumbs-down. Only Joshua and Caleb came back with a thumbs-up. The risk assessment from the other ten frightened the nation of Israel so much that they rebelled against God's promise and almost killed Caleb and Joshua. God had promised, but the people were not willing to trust Him or His Word. Where did they end up? Wandering in the wilderness for forty years.

Forty years. That's about the length of time a modern man spends in the workforce. That's about two thousand weeks (if a man takes off two weeks per year for vacation). That's about eighty thousand hours plus overtime. (That's worth thinking about. If you're giving your life to your job, it better be worth eighty thousand of your best hours.)

Forty years was long enough for an entire generation to die off. None of the ten doubting surveyors would set foot in the Promised Land again. But Caleb remembered what he had seen, and he still saw it through the eyes of God's promise. *"My companions who went with me discouraged the people, but I stuck to my guns totally with God, my God"* (Joshua 14:8 MSG). Moses solemnly promised, *"The land on which your feet have walked will be your inheritance and that of your children forever"* (Joshua 14:9). When all was said and done, after forty years of wandering, Caleb and Joshua were the only two of the entire generation who were allowed to enter into the Promised Land.

Their children and their children's children received the benefit of their fathers' faithfulness to God. God spoke about the people and then about Caleb. He said,

> *Not one of them will set eyes on the land I solemnly promised to their ancestors. No one who has treated me with such repeated contempt will see it. But my servant Caleb—this is a different story. He has a different spirit; he follows me passionately. I'll bring him into the land that he scouted, and his children will inherit it.*
>
> (Numbers 14:23–24 MSG)

I love that verse. Caleb had *"a **different spirit**; he follows me passionately"* (verse 24, emphasis added). There *was* something different about Caleb and Joshua. God tells us exactly what it was: these two had heard the promises of God, and they adjusted their lives to those truths. They took the risk; they followed God fully. It was a risk, no question about that. There were plenty of people who warned them to play it safe. That advice cost a generation their lives. Only the two that obeyed in faith, despite the risk assessment involved, were allowed to enter into the life that God had promised the people in the Promised Land.

MAKING THE CONNECTION

Your ability to take your one shot at life, trusting the promises of God, not only affects you but determines the future of your family. In fact, the destiny of your family is dependent on your willingness to risk taking God at His word. To live by faith and not by sight is the beginning of an adventure to honor God.

If a man really believed that God loved him, how could this make him courageous beyond reason? What kinds of risks might he be willing to take?

There comes a time when the things that we say we believe must be acted upon—not with an outward action, but with an action that begins in the heart as we embrace everything that God says is true and allow those truths to begin working their way towards our outward lives. It's a critical moment, a defining moment, and critical questions must be answered in our hearts:

Is Scripture *really* true?

Is Christ *really* real?

Does Father God *really* love me like a perfect Father loves his sons?

Is true life *really* found in Christ?

Does Christ *really* exist in my spirit?

Have I *really* died and experienced new life in Christ?

The Challenge to Risk it All

If you've been in church for any length of time, these are things you can probably answer in your head. They might be things that you've been taught since you were a child. But are you willing to take a risk? Are you willing to step out and begin to live in a way that is consistent with the things that you say you believe?

There's risk in that, isn't there? There is an assessment to be made. Jesus encouraged men to count the cost in any venture, and He never assumed that the answer would be an easy "yes." He's still calling us today to count the cost and risk it all on the promise of His Word. He calls for the kind of belief that leads to a changed life, not just some kind of theological statement. He didn't claim that we wouldn't face fear in the process. In the Scriptures, the issue of fear is addressed 365 times. (That's once for every day of the year!) Clearly, God knows that this will be a continual enemy.

God also knows that there will be people out there—sometimes well-meaning people—who will try to keep us from taking risks. They will say, "You can't really believe everything in the Bible. There is no value in risking everything. You have to be reasonable because that's what men should be: careful and cautious." Sometimes the voice of unbelief says, "Remember, there are giants in the land, and you are a grasshopper."

Many men have faced such unbelief. There is a great illustration of this in the movie *Rudy*. As a child, "Rudy" Ruettiger began to dream of playing football at Notre Dame, but the obstacles he faced seemed impossible to overcome. He was small; he was from the wrong side of the tracks; he struggled as a student… but he was also undeterred. Those who tried to protect him from failure could not quench the dream. One of those people was his own father. As Rudy stood in the bus station waiting to chase his "calling," his dad tried to talk him out of taking the risk: "Chasing a stupid dream causes nothing but you and everyone around you heartache. Notre Dame is for rich kids, smart kids, great athletes. It's not for us! You're a Ruettiger."[7]

Rudy got on the bus.

What God-inspired dream has been placed in your heart?

The road to his dream was brutal, but, in the final game of his senior year, Rudy got to dress out with the team. In the last seconds of the game, Rudy was sent onto the field. On the last play, Rudy made the final tackle to end game. He was the only player in the history of the school to be carried off the field by his teammates.

Awesome movie. True story.

We admire guys like Rudy, like Caleb…like Evel Knievel…and for good reason. Men like these are free, strong, and they have purpose and direction. They symbolize the essence of what we long to be—a longing that God has given each of us deep inside.

ESSENTIAL RISK

Consider what we've discussed so far. We've established the reliability and validity of God's Word. We have searched for and discovered the loving heart of an eternal, all-powerful Father God. We've embraced this love and begun to make it our own. By doing so, we have received and recognized the incredible promises that God has given to those who believe. By His own actions, as an expression of who He is, God has forgiven us, made us pure, and adopted us as His children.

THE CHALLENGE TO RISK IT ALL

These are His promises. His Word tells us they're true. The question is, *Are you willing to "possess" or enter into the land?* The answer to that question makes the difference between wandering in the desert for the next forty years or embracing the vibrant, dynamic, purpose-filled life that God intends you to live.

The Bible says, *"It is for freedom that Christ has set us free. Stand firm, then, and do not let yourselves be burdened again by a yoke of slavery"* (Galatians 5:1). The choice is yours: slavery to the *bios* life and its fears; or freedom through embracing the unconditional love of the Father.

Apart from faith, you will never experience what you were created for; you will never experience the fulfillment of the desires God Himself has placed within your heart.

The ultimate risky loss, then, is actually a life wasted in fear. What if you were to risk it all on the fact that Scripture is true, that God's love is a reality, and that you are who He says you are: a beloved son? What if you seized the promise that life—true life—is found in Christ and Christ in us, rather than in the things of the world?

At some point, the knowing must stop and the faith that produces action must begin. I'm not necessarily talking about great outward acts of faith. The adventure of risking it all begins in the depths of the heart. From there, it makes its way to the outward aspects of our lives. But make no mistake: the outward adventure begins by embracing what God says is inwardly true about us. Risking it all on God might very well cost us everything someday—perhaps even life itself. But what is the alternative? That we live lives that are supposedly safe, secure, and predictable? Are we ever really safe or secure apart from taking God at His word?

ONE SHOT

Do we have any assurances about our lives apart from a relationship with Christ?

Inside of each of us lurks the spirit of a small boy—the one who wants to fly like Evel Knievel. The boy is older now, but he is still there…and he knows it's time to make the jump.

RISK ASSESSMENT

▶ List three risks that you need to take to in order to realize your dreams.

▶ What fears are attached to the following risks? How do they affect you?

- Fear of Failure
- Fear of Rejection
- Fear of Being Real
- Fear of Death

▶ If you were to take a risk anyway, what do you have to lose? That's not a throwaway question. Write down the possible losses you might face if you risk it all.

THE REWARDS OF RISK

► **Matthew 10:28**

Don't be bluffed into silence by the threats of bullies. There's nothing they can do to your soul, your core being. Save your fear for God, who holds your entire life—body and soul—in his hands.

► **Psalm 27:1**

Light, space, zest—that's God! So, with him on my side I'm fearless, afraid of no one and nothing.

► **Mark 4:40**

Jesus reprimanded the disciples: "Why are you such cowards? Don't you have any faith at all?"

RISKING IT ALL ON THE PROMISES OF GOD

In the year 1776, the founding fathers of the United States of America took a risk. Looking back, we know that they were men of great courage and valor. But these men also faced very strong fears. The day that they stood around the table and signed the Declaration of Independence, they were fully aware that they had just signed their own death warrant. It was a statement of rebellion and treason against the powers that existed. Should the rebellion fail, they were all to face the firing squad or the gallows. Fear did not deter them.

The Challenge to Risk it All

Their lives were fueled by a vision for something new and something different...something free. They had assessed the risks, looked at the possibilities, considered the implications this would have for their families, and they believed. As men of God, we now stand on the verge of a parallel declaration...

The Declaration of Independence from Fear

When in the course of human events, it becomes necessary for one man to dissolve the emotional bondage which has connected him to fear, and to assume, among the Powers of the earth, that the truth and presence of God promises freedom from such fear. I hold these truths to be evident in Scripture, that I am created, that I have been endowed by my Creator with full rights as His adopted son, and that the blood of Christ has purchased for me life, liberty, and the pursuit of His holiness. That whenever any entity becomes destructive of these ends, it is the right of the man to alter or to abolish it and to institute new boundaries in his soul, laying its foundation on such principles and organizing its powers in such form as to reflect truth as defined in the Holy Scriptures. I claim my independence from these specific fears:

Therefore, as an ambassador of Jesus Christ, I claim His authority over these fears, and for the support of this Declaration, with a firm reliance on the protection of divine providence, pledge myself to the adventure of risking it all, that I might know the power of Christ in me, for the sake of each others' lives, our families, and our sacred honor.

Signed,

Dear God, I will not be afraid to believe Your Word and stand on the statements of truth found there. Let my heart always be open to You and move in faith that You're always watching over me. Help me to be courageous—to risk my life and the life of my family on Your promises. When I pray, I know that You hear me and will move on my behalf. In Jesus' name, amen.

SECTION III
SIGNIFICANCE

Significance (sĭg-nĭf'ĭ-kəns) *n.* The state or quality of being engaged in something important or of great consequence or meaning.

In this section, we unleash the truths of the last two sections in three vitally important areas:

1) Connecting with other men,

2) Engaging the heart of a woman, and

3) Leaving a legacy that will stand the test of time.

The significance of these areas of a Promise Keeper's life make a huge difference as he strives to take his one shot at life, making it count for things that truly matter.

Women now have choices. They can be married, not married, have a job, not have a job, be married with children, unmarried with children. Men have the same choice we've always had: work or prison.

—*Tim Allen*

Try not to become a man of success, but rather try to become a man of value.

—*Albert Einstein*

Ultimately, we're all dead men. Sadly, we cannot choose how, but what we can decide is how we meet that end, in order that we are remembered as men.

—*Proximo,* Gladiator

This is where they fought the battle of Gettysburg. Fifty thousand men died right here on this field, fighting the same fight that we are still fighting among ourselves today.... Listen to their souls, men. "I killed my brother with malice in my heart. Hatred destroyed my family." You listen, and you take a lesson from the dead. If we don't come together right now on this hallowed ground, we too will be destroyed, just like they were.

—*Coach Boone,* Remember the Titans

Let us consider how to stimulate one another to love and good deeds, not forsaking our own assembling together, as is the habit of some, but encouraging one another; and all the more as you see the day drawing near.

—*Hebrews 10:24–25* (NASB)

CHAPTER 7

I WAS READING THROUGH E-mails and deleting spam this week when I received a message from an old friend. At first, I was excited to hear from him, but the news he had to share was a complete shock.

Subject: News from a friend

Todd,

I hope this e-mail finds you doing well. I know it has been a long time since we've spoken. I apologize for that. In many regards, I feel very selfish writing to you—in what you will soon learn is an hour of need. I have not been a real good friend in terms of keeping up with you (personally)—and I am sorry for that....I have some very sad news to send your way. My wife told me this week she has her mind made up to pursue a divorce. It has been a very troubling week—as this is not at all my desire. This is 100 percent her decision—and one that she says she is at peace with God to make.

I would ask that you pray for me. I am not doing very well right now. Life is dark, full of uncertainty, fear, pain, and despair. I am numb. I am in shock. I thought we had made a lifelong commitment to each other. I confess to being confused and do not understand how that commitment is seemingly no longer applicable.

Please pray for me. I know I have made mistakes. I have not been faithful in growing with her over the past several years. I was lazy—oftentimes overwhelmed with the day-to-day challenges of raising a family, working a job—and I took her for granted in many regards. Pray that God would pierce my heart with an understanding of where I need to repent in my relationship with Him. Pray that God would give me strength to get through these days….

I am asking you this favor because I know you are a man of faith and that it is biblical to have people petitioning God on your behalf. Please my brother, pray for a miracle. Pray that God would be pleased to save this marriage—and that Satan would not win this battle for this home.

Pray that it stays a home.

I love you, respect you—and would appreciate this favor more than you know.

The Significance of Connecting with a Few Other Men

The news came like a solid punch in the gut. I reached for the phone and dialed his number. *How could this be?* I had been in his wedding. I stood up with him and his wife as they made their vows. I promised to support their marriage to the best of my ability...but our lives had been separated by six hundred miles and seven years.

I heard his voice on the other end, broken and exhausted. As the story unfolded, I began to understand: No connection with Christian men. No brothers to encourage, support, and battle for his marriage. He was going to church, but where were the men in his life to help him and his wife continue in their vows? There was none. He was standing alone.

CONNECTION POINT

Connected. We need to be connected. It's essential in times of difficulty and struggle. In those moments, men need to reach out to those who are closest to them—those they can count on.

An isolated man is a vulnerable man, an easy pickoff for the enemy of his soul. We need those who will walk beside us, speak truth into our lives, laugh with us, and cry with us when necessary. Our culture seems to honor the man standing alone against injustice. In truth, no man stands alone who stands at all.

How connected are you to other men of faith?

What does it mean for men to connect authentically—in Christ—with one another? First of all, it means risk. To be connected means to be locked arm in arm, to be dependent, to be transparent. To be transparent means you have take a risk—the risk of being honest and possibly misunderstood. Some men have experienced difficult outcomes from past attempts to connect, but the examples of men connecting in Scripture can motivate us to try it again and to try it differently.

One of the most amazing examples of men connecting with each other is found in 1 Samuel 18. Here we see the remarkable relationship between Jonathan and David. This relationship had every reason to be strained and disconnected. Jonathan was the son of the current King of Israel, and David was the nation's greatest warrior and eventual King. You'd think that there would be hostility between the two—or at least some competition—but the exact opposite took place. They became *"one in spirit"* (1 Samuel 18:1). Each of them loved the other as himself.

How would you describe your closest friendships with other men? Where are they strongest?

The story of their lives soon took an incredible twist that led them on a trail of life-and-death encounters. Jonathan's father, King Saul, tried to have David killed, and at one point he even tried to get Jonathan to do it. But Jonathan warned David instead, telling him to be on his guard and go into hiding from his father's fury. The bond between them held, and the connection between Jonathan and David extended over the course of their lives...and even into the lives of their children.

Jonathan was eventually killed in battle, while David became King of Israel. Jonathan left behind a crippled son, who was fearful that King David would try to kill him because his grandfather was the late King Saul. But when David found out that the son of Jonathan was alive, he took him in as his own son. David told him, in essence, "Your home is with me, because you were the son of my best friend, Jonathan." (See 2 Samuel 9.)

The Significance of Connecting with a Few Other Men

Connecting with other men breaks down barriers, as well. The disciples were a phenomenal example of how a diverse group of men can be drawn together if they have a common bond in Jesus Christ. Look at these guys' credentials: some were fishermen; one was a tax collector; another was a political activist; some were rich and some were poor; they came from every segment of society. But they came together with bonds so strong that many of them walked willingly into death together for the cause of Jesus Christ.

What does it mean to spur each other on in Christ in order to become the men God created us to be? It's critically important that we find the answer. But going at it alone will never be that answer.

MOSTLY ALONE

Recent research quoted in David Murrow's book *Why Men Hate Going to Church* indicates that men are increasingly distancing themselves from their local churches:

- This Sunday almost 25 percent of married, churchgoing women will worship without their husbands.

- As many as 90 percent of the boys who are being raised in church will abandon it by their twentieth birthday. Many of these boys will never return.

- More than 90 percent of American men believe in God, and five out of six call themselves Christians. But only two out of six attend church on a given Sunday. The average man accepts the reality of Jesus Christ but fails to see any value in going to church.

- A significant number of churchgoing men attend out of habit, unaffected by what they hear.

- Quite a few men go to church simply to keep their wives, mothers, or girlfriends happy.
- The majority of men who attend church do nothing during the week to grow in their faith.
- Relatively few churches are able to establish or maintain a vibrant men's ministry.[8]

Patrick Morley's research has come to similar conclusions. As he states in his book *No Man Left Behind*, out of every ten men in a local church:

- Nine will have children who leave the church.
- Eight will not find satisfying jobs.
- Six will pay the monthly minimum on their credit card bills.
- Five will have a major problem with pornography.
- Four will get divorced, affecting one million children every year.
- Only one will have a biblical worldview.
- All ten will struggle to balance work and family.[9]

BEYOND THE PEW

Jesus had no trouble captivating or connecting with men. Fishermen dropped nets full of fish to follow Him. Tax collectors left their livelihood to assist Him. Zealots pledged to die for Him. Men, great and small, devoted their lives to Him. Beyond this first generation of followers of Christ, history tells of men who brazenly worshipped God and participated in the life of the local church. They had no buildings, no organs, no midweek programs...and yet this "church" was indestructible. It seemed to multiply spontaneously as if it had a life of its own.

The Significance of Connecting with a Few Other Men

And it did have a life of its own. The believers focused all of their energy and passions on the reality of Jesus Christ in themselves and in each other. They supported each other, forgave each other, and carried each other's burdens. They labored together, laughed together, and grieved together. In difficult times, they even believed for each other, supporting each other through seasons of doubt and confronting each other in love when necessary. It was largely unstructured, it was not focused in any one location, and it grew like crazy. It was the *"body of Christ"* (1 Corinthians 12:27). Men were connected with each other as men, focused on the common cause of Jesus. Throughout the centuries, many have sustained this level of simple, unhindered fellowship. A spontaneous synergy erupts when this kind of brotherhood is experienced.

I remember the night I left with a bunch of friends for a rustic cabin and an evening getaway. Things went very well until the sun went down and everything started to cool off. The firewood we had collected was still pretty fresh, and we soon found out that blue lips and green wood is not a good combination; we couldn't get the darn stuff to light.

Paper didn't seem to be a sufficient igniter, so some of us figured that we needed to step it up a little bit. I figured that the problem could be easily solved with a match and some gasoline siphoned from our car. Some of the other guys figured differently. They had this crazy notion that igniting an explosive liquid in a confined space could turn our quaint little cabin into a big bomb.

We actually got upset with one another. We had some strong things to say to each other as well. Thankfully, the night ended quite uneventfully. The others eventually talked us down from the ridiculous idea. We spent the rest of the night freezing our tails off but sharing into the wee hours of the morning.

We went to the mountains to get away and ended up getting real instead.

In the 1990s, Promise Keepers began encouraging men to meet regularly in small groups of three to five for prayer, encouragement, and Bible study. Today, many of these groups continue to gather in coffee shops, churches, restaurants, and workplaces. Numerous men's groups provide support structures that have prompted lifelong friendships, authentic communication, and spiritual maturity.

The command we have from Christ is blunt: Loving God includes loving people. You've got to love both. (1 John 4:21 MSG)

We definitely see the need to connect, but how does a man become authentically connected to a few other brothers in Christ?

SOME WHO HAVE GONE BEFORE US

The war was on. Amalek was attacking Israel. Joshua had men by his side and was engaging the enemy. On a hill overlooking the battlefield, Moses stood with his arms raised high. While Moses kept his arms raised, the battle belonged to the armies of Israel. But when his arms began to come down, the enemy would advance against the people of God. As the battle continued, it became impossible for Moses to stand alone. The strength of two other men, Aaron and Hur, covered for his weakness, holding Moses' arms up and giving him the strength he needed to complete the task God had given him. The battle would belong to Israel.

The Significance of Connecting with a Few Other Men

Throughout our lives, there are moments, hours, and seasons when we must stand together; if we don't, we will fail. This is part of God's design. He designed us to work in unison with each other, doing together what cannot be done alone. Connecting with a few men helps each of us accomplish the calling and purpose of God in each man. We become a team, a platoon, with each person functioning in his strengths to cover the backs of those around him.

Do you know what you can do to help the men around you fulfill their God-given callings?

Men in such groups ask this question: "How am I helping you live out your calling?" Our role isn't as much keeping each other in line and out of trouble as it is encouraging and equipping each other to fight the good fight. Successful groups know that *strength is multiplied and complemented when men of Christ come together in His name.* As men, we aren't policing each other; we are looking for ways to encourage each other to take risks based on the promises of God. Our goal becomes clear: we must energize our brothers, help them see themselves as God sees them, and encourage and equip them as men of valor and vision.

Though one may be overpowered, two can defend themselves. A cord of three strands is not quickly broken. (Ecclesiastes 4:12)

Men bond around a common cause. It might be business; it might be a sports team; it might be a hobby; it might be a war.... This is just part of our natural design. A special bond is formed when men are connected and committed to a cause. Relationships that last are always built around things that last. When Christian men come together with a passion for what God has done in their lives, there is a strength and energy that overflows into each other's lives. One man's weakness is covered by another man's strength.

The desire to be together seems to be strongest in times of great emotional need. In Matthew 26:36–45, we see Jesus in the garden of Gethsemane, knowing that He will soon face torture and death. He took Peter, James, and John along with Him to pray. As the weight of the situation descended on His heart, He said to these men, *"My soul is overwhelmed with sorrow to the point of death. Stay here and keep watch with me"* (verse 38). Jesus, in the midst of His most difficult hour, wanted His friends to come a little further with Him and pray as He faced His destiny.

Second Timothy is the final letter we have from Paul. It too is an impassioned cry to a friend by one who knows that he has reached the end of his life. He seeks out the fellowship of his brothers in Christ as he faces his execution: *"I have fought the good fight....Do your best to come to me quickly....get here before winter"* (2 Timothy 4: 7, 9, 21).

We need this kind of support; we were made for this kind of brotherhood. We need the perspective that comes from men who are engaged in our lives. We need the strength that comes from men who can speak the truth of God's Word to us. Oftentimes, we need encouragement to hang on to what we know is true. We need men in our lives who know our histories—men who can speak to us, reminding us of God's loving-kindness and faithfulness.

This is *real* fellowship. It can happen in a living room, in a coffee shop, on a golf course, or in a church sanctuary. Connecting with men happens when guys who understand the truth gather together to joyfully share their journey into the heart of God. This bond emerges among men who are committed to one another, who live their lives together, and who are astounded by who they are in Christ.

Yes, brotherhood happens when a few men come together around the common goal of sharing the love of God—and since God is love, what they're really sharing with each other is God Himself. As an extension of who Christ is in them, they also celebrate and give each other grace and mercy. When men connect with each other in this way, they're really connecting with the Spirit of Christ who is in each of them! That's a wild thought, I know. But it's the same kind of unity and oneness that Christ prayed for:

> *Holy Father, protect them by the power of your name—the name that you gave me—so that they may be one as we are one....that all of them may be one, Father, just as you are in me and I am in you. May they be also be in us so that the world may believe that you have sent me....I in them and you and me. May they be brought to complete unity to the let the world know that you sent me and have loved them even as you have loved me.* (John 17:11, 21, 23)

PART OF A GREATER TEAM

While we can have the pleasure of being a part of what God is doing in the lives of other men, we can in no way take credit for it—I learned this graphically not long ago. (I'm still a little dazed when I think about how God worked this out. If it hadn't happened to me, I doubt I would have believed it.)

I was running for the State Senate and raising money for my campaign everywhere I could. Financing a campaign is just one of the harsh realities of politics. (After awhile, my friends began answering the phone, "Hi Todd, I've already given.")

One day my good friend and brother in Christ, Doug Meduna, came to my office and pulled me aside. "You know, Todd, I want to talk to you," he said with a serious tone. I was immediately concerned. Doug has been the leader of my small group Bible study for many years. He was the one that initiated our group by connecting a handful of men who had common interests. We started hanging out together and something clicked. Now we meet every other Saturday night with our families for dinner, laughter, some Bible time, and lots of just hanging out. A respectful bond has been built between us, so when Doug said he wanted to talk, I was ready to listen.

"I just want to tell you that I've been thinking and praying about the way you're raising money. I think that something in that process is not honoring the Lord," he said.

"Really?" I said. "I don't know what else to do, Doug. I obviously do not want to offend the Lord. What do I change?"

"I can't tell you that," Doug said. "I don't know what you should do. There is just something about the fund-raising that does not seem right to me, and I believe I was supposed to share that with you."

I know Doug loves and respects me. I was grateful that he cared enough to share those difficult words. I began to pray that God would show me what I was to do differently, because I didn't know how to practically address his concerns.

Fast-forward to New York City four weeks later. I was at the last crusade that Billy Graham would ever lead. There was an enormous crowd of people attending along with presidents, well-known personalities, pastors, and, well, me. I happened to have four extra backstage passes in my pocket that some of our

The Significance of Connecting with a Few Other Men

company's senior staff members at Integrity Music were unable to use at the last minute. As I mingled in the crowd, I noticed a woman looking directly at me. She began to walk in my direction. She did not introduce herself; she simply said, "I was standing over there praying, and God told me that you had four additional tickets. I want to ask you for them."

I was stunned.

"Ma'am," I said in a startled voice, "I have no idea who you are, but these four tickets obviously belong to you. Can I ask who they are for?" I thought she said that they were for her pastor and family. I gave her the tickets and my card. "Would you mind having your pastor give me a call?" I asked.

Fast-forward about three more weeks. I received a call from the respected pastor Harold Bredesen. "Hello," he said in a kind voice. "I'm calling to say that God provided those tickets in such a wonderful and unusual way."

"Yes sir," I said. "It was my honor." We talked for awhile, and, as he was about to hang up, I asked him to pray for me and the campaign. There was a long pause on the other end of the line. I waited…and waited a little bit longer.

"Todd," he finally said, "I want to tell you some things before we pray. The first is that you have questions about how you are asking people for money. The problem is not *how* you're asking; it's that you have placed your hope in men providing for your financial needs. You need to know that God is your source. He will provide."

Tears welled up in my eyes, and a knot filled my throat. He was right. It wasn't the process of asking for money that was wrong. It was my unbelief. I had come to believe that if I could raise enough money from other men, I could win. Of course, God can do with one dollar what men cannot do with a billion dollars. As soon as I heard Pastor Bredesen's words, I knew that God was calling me to a deeper fellowship with Him through repentance.

When was the last time a close friend gave you an honest critique of your actions or questioned your motives? How did you respond?

How was I to explain what had just happened? Not only had God answered my prayers, but He had done it in a way that made the message absolutely clear: God works through teams of individuals in our lives. No one has to try to do it all alone. God used a brother in Alabama, an unknown woman in New York, and a distinguished pastor calling from Boston to minister truth in my life. That's the love of a Father: to correct us and use fellowship with others to communicate His purposes.

That was a good lesson and a life-changing experience for me. God can accomplish His work in any way He chooses. As part of the greater body of Christ, each one of us is responsible for pursing the things that lead to peace and the building up of one another. (See Romans 14:19.) God is fully capable, and He works through us as a body to accomplish His work.

This is a vital truth to bring home to our small groups and friendships. We don't have to be the Holy Spirit to each other. He can use any means He wishes to accomplish His goals in each of our lives. We can rest. We can trust. We can listen and obey when He calls us to move or to speak. Yet we must always trust God for the results and for lives of those we love. We don't have to fix things ourselves or have answers for every question.

The Significance of Connecting with a Few Other Men

Men who know this will be vibrant and alive. The pressure and manipulation often associated with "accountability groups" will disappear. We will be free to allow the Spirit of God to work through us in any way that He sees fit. Together, by connecting with a few other men who understand these principles and want to pursue God, we will experience the life of Christ in new ways.

And the significance of that cannot be overstated.

RISK ASSESSMENT

▶ What are some of the potential dangers of connecting with a few other men?

▶ In your opinion, what would be the result of a group where the members try to police one another?

▶ What are some of the dangers of *not* connecting with a few other men?

▶ Are you in conflict with men that you need to forgive and be in right relationships with? Are you willing to initiate this call?

THE REWARDS OF RISK

▶ **Romans 12:15–16**

*Laugh with your happy friends when they're happy; share
tears when they're down. Get along with each other; don't
be stuck-up. Make friends with nobodies; don't be the great
somebody.*

▶ **Jude 22–23**

*Go easy on those who hesitate in the faith. Go after those who
take the wrong way. Be tender with sinners, but not soft on sin.
The sin itself stinks to high heaven.*

▶ **Proverbs 22:24–25**

*Don't hang out with angry people; don't keep company with
hotheads. Bad temper is contagious—don't get infected.*

RISKING IT ALL ON CONNECTING
WITH A FEW OTHER MEN

Pick up the phone and call a couple like-minded friends. Get everybody together for breakfast, lunch, or an afternoon of hiking, golf, etc. Don't make a big deal about it. Just pray about it, get together, and see what happens. Pick up the phone—today.

The Significance of Connecting with a Few Other Men

Heavenly Father, let me experience the fellowship and shared life that You have for me with other men. Allow Your Holy Spirit to lead me in positive relationships with men that help me understand Your ways. Thank You for the fellowship that comes from knowing You. Thank You for the men whom You have called to stand and walk beside me. In Jesus' precious name, amen.

Marriage is a fine institution, but who wants
to live in an institution?

—*Bob Cole*

The great living experience for every man
is his adventure into the woman. The man
embraces in the woman all that is not himself,
and from that one resultant, from that
embrace, comes every new action.

—*D. H. Lawrence*

Marriage is our last, best chance to grow up.

—*Joseph Barth*

To keep your marriage brimming,
With love in the loving cup,
Whenever you're wrong admit it;
Whenever you're right shut up.

—*Ogden Nash*

[Marriage] *is a huge mystery, and I don't
pretend to understand it all.*

—*The apostle Paul,
Ephesians 5:32* (MSG)

CHAPTER 8

BACK IN THE DAY, TO MAKE some extra money during college, I was a wedding singer. This was before Adam Sandler's movie made guys like me look glamorous. One time, I was singing "The Lord's Prayer." The bride and groom were kneeling together, absorbed in the moment. The ring bearer was a chunky little tank; he wore a size "husky," just like I did when I was a kid. Anyway, he must have locked his knees or forgotten to breathe or something because, in the middle of the song, he passed out cold and did a header right into the bride and groom. Took them out like a bowling ball. Stuff went flying everywhere.

His dad was a big ol' country boy—a grown-up version of the kid. He jumped up on stage, picked up the boy by one leg, carried him off the platform, and dragged him out a side door just as I was singing "Amen"…and the wedding kept on going as if nothing happened. In fact, if you had been praying with your eyes closed, you would have missed the whole show. You'd have opened your eyes and wondered where the heck Junior went.

In another wedding, they had asked me to sing five songs right in the middle of the ceremony. I had told them this wasn't a good idea, but they were writing my check, so I went with it. By the end of the third song, the audience had had more than enough of me; the groom could sense this and decided to take matters into his own hands. The dude walked over to the piano, took the mike, and asked me if I knew the song "Lady" by Lionel Richie. It was probably the only song he thought he could sing. He slaughtered it. Really bad. The women loved it, of course.

I've always given that guy high marks for being a man of action, but he found out the hard way that singing a solo in front of a hundred people is just a pinch different from singing in the car with the radio on high and the windows rolled down.

MEN OF ACTION

I think we are all like that guy in some ways. We are men of action. We want to fix stuff. When it comes to women, we've got good hearts but sometimes overestimate our own abilities to get the job done. We might get high marks for bravery, but our efforts can be all over the place.

The heart of a woman is a mysterious frontier; I realize that. But in today's world, how does a man intent on following Jesus understand a woman's heart and also relate to her honorably, respectfully, purely, and with godly strength? There are answers to these questions—very good answers. In fact, they apply not only to our marriages but also to our daughters and the women in our churches and workplaces.

"He who finds a wife finds a good thing" (Proverbs 18:22 NKJV). Are you single? God still has a lot to say to you about how to relate to women; but because relational intensity is turned up in

marriage, that's the relationship that we're going to focus on now. (Just know that biblical principles are extremely valuable in any relationship that you have, even if it's not a romantic one.)

FIRST THINGS FIRST

Where do we start to understand God's unique design of a woman's heart and how a godly man should engage that heart? Believe it or not, we *don't* start with action…at least not quite yet. I know how hard it is not to jump right in; after all, we are designed to be men of action. However, the things we need to talk about go much deeper than our actions. We're talking about issues of the heart—engaging the heart of a woman—and if *your* heart isn't in the right place, all your efforts are going to go south, no matter what you do. So before we run off to sing love songs outside her window, we need to make sure we understand two principles.

Principle one: *Jesus Christ is your life, your* Zoë *life; your wife is not your life.* You are one flesh; you are to experience intimacy with her like you do with no other, but she cannot be the primary source of your meaning and fulfillment in life. That's Jesus' place.

Physically and emotionally, men are hardwired to desire the affection and respect of women. Initially, we will always be attracted to the physical rather than the spiritual to fulfill our needs. This is certainly the case when it comes to marriage. A good marriage is like the frosting on a cake, but it's not the cake. If you focus on the frosting, you're never going to find the true fulfillment and meaning that you desire in your relationships. That's why your Zoë life has to come from your relationship with Jesus Christ: because Jesus *is* your life. He's the cake.

If you believe that your wife is here to serve you and satisfy your needs, you are going down a very dangerous road. She wasn't designed to meet your needs. She will never completely fulfill you, no matter how much she gives or how much you get...and that includes sex too. My friend was talking through some difficult issues with a young couple recently. They were going through some tough times, and the topic of sex came up over and over again. The husband wanted more; the wife felt like she had nothing left to give. "How often do you guys have sexual intimacy?" he asked. The guy looked at him and said, "Three times a day."

I don't normally laugh at people's problems. That day was an exception. This guy was experiencing the frosting—*a lot* of frosting. But it still wasn't enough. It's never enough to look to anything else but Christ to complete us.

Principle two: *Jesus Christ wants to love your wife through you, just as He loves the church.*

Can you think of times when you expected your wife to meet your deepest personal needs?

I can't tell you how important this is. If you don't recognize that Christ is the only One who can strengthen and grow your marriage, then you have missed the point of this book. If you run out there and try to love your wife by "making it work" on your own, "doing what you've got to do," or simply telling yourself "it can wait," then disappointment awaits you.

The only way this works is to allow God to love your wife through you. Remember: "*We love because he first loved us*" (1 John 4:19). Without Him, "*you can do nothing*" (John 15:5). Through the strength of Christ, "*you can do everything*" (Philippians 4:13). Even if your marriage is really struggling, even if you don't feel like there is hope, even if you're in need of forgiveness, even if she has left you, *all things* are still possible.

Is trusting Christ in this way risky? Of course it is. We have to trust that Christ can love our wives better than we can. Then we have to give up and allow Him to do it. That's not easy for a man, but, thankfully, God has shown us exactly what this looks like.

CHRIST AND THE CHURCH / YOU AND YOUR WIFE

All right, we're getting closer to the "doing" part (but not quite yet). We know that the only way we can fully engage the heart of a woman is through Christ. But how do we do this? We follow the model of Christ's love for us and the church:

> *Husbands, go all out in your love for your wives, exactly as Christ did for the church—a love marked by giving, not getting. Christ's love makes the church whole. His words evoke her beauty. Everything he does and says is designed to bring the best out of her, dressing her in dazzling white silk, radiant with holiness. And that is how husbands ought to love their wives. They're really doing themselves a favor—since they're already "one" in marriage. No one abuses his own body, does he? No, he feeds and pampers it. That's how Christ treats us, the church, since we are part of his body. And this is why a man leaves father and mother and cherishes his wife. No longer two, they become "one flesh." This is a huge mystery, and I don't pretend to understand it all. What is clearest to me is the way Christ treats the church. And this provides a good picture of how each husband is to treat his wife, loving himself in loving her, and how each wife is to honor her husband.*
>
> (Ephesians 5:25–33 MSG)

That's a loaded passage. It almost seems like Paul is confused. In one sentence, he's talking about marriage; in the next sentence, he's talking about Christ and the church. And then he bounces back again. Which is it? It's both! The way Christ loves the church is the way we are to love our wives. There's something mysterious going on here, and the parallels are striking.

A Covenant

As the ultimate Promise Keeper, God is very serious about the commitments He makes. He uses a special word to describe them; He calls them "covenants." When God made a covenant with Abram (see Genesis 15), He took animals and cut them in half. Their blood was spilled between the two halves, and God walked through the middle of those animals as if to say, "If I do not keep My covenant, may it be done unto Me as it was with these animals." God is serious about keeping His covenants.

In your marriage vows, you made a covenant with your wife. The covenant is not just between you and your wife; it's a covenant that the two of you made before God and with God. *Your* marriage is *God's* idea. No matter the circumstances surrounding your marriage, God's purposes for marriage are still in effect. He can take any marriage—even one that seems like a "mistake"— and transform it into something wonderful and useful for His purposes. We know this because God is always good, loving, and in control.

Forgiveness

The forgiveness of God is the *only* thing that allows us to continue in a relationship with Him. God tells us in His Word that He has removed our sins *"as far as the east is from the west"* (Psalm 103:12), and that He *"will remember their sins no more"* (Jeremiah

The Significance of Engaging the Heart of a Woman

31:34). This means that we are forgiven, and God will not hold our sins over our heads in anger. His mercy and grace will cover every sin in our lives, and He won't bring up the past once we're forgiven.

And this is the way that we are to forgive our wives—the way that Christ forgives us. "Impossible!" you say. "That's right," the Bible says. You can't do this, but Christ can do it through you. If you surrender your anger and frustration and bitterness to God, you can allow Him to forgive your wife for what she has done or not done. Then you will be free to love again, and she just might become free to receive your love...just as we are free to receive His love.

Pursuit

God has always pursued us with His love. We don't have to chase God down. This is part of discovering the heart of God: we discover that His heart is always available, always willing, and always in pursuit of our love and commitment.

What hurts do you need to forgive your wife for? What offenses do you need to ask her forgiveness for?

Pastor Frank Barker Jr. has had a great influence on me. He is an ex–Navy fighter pilot and the former pastor of a large, influential church where he served God for many years. In the book *Flight Path,* he shares how God pursued him even as he tried to run far from Him. Driving on a gravel road late one night, Frank fell asleep at the wheel, and the car went spinning out of control. When his car stopped, this is what he remembers:

> The countryside night was dark as pitch. As the
> dust began to settle, I looked up and I saw my
> headlights shine on something large and white

right in front of my car. It was a big sign nailed on a tree. What it said shocked me more than my near fatal accident. I would remember the words on that sign all my life. In large black letters was written "The Wages of Sin Is Death." I thought, *Good grief, I don't believe this is an accident. I think God let me go to sleep and stop right in front of this sign. He's trying to tell me something....*[10]

It was God in pursuit of his heart. There are countless stories about people who have been pursued by God. I am one of them. So are you. Anyone who has come to faith in Christ has a similar story. Together we make up the story of the entire church. We have all been loved and pursued by God. He pursued us from our infancy and before we were even born. He continues to pursue us through our mistakes, failures, and shortcomings. He pursues us at this very moment.

And that's the way we are supposed to pursue the hearts of our wives: lovingly, persistently, and regardless of their responses.

Remember that you are pursuing a relationship, and, just like our relationship with God, it's not based on performance. If your efforts are part of a checklist that proves you've done your job, it will backfire. We all know the difference between duty and devotion. Marriage is not 50 percent get and 50 percent give. It's actually 100 percent: you get 100 percent of your life from Christ, and you give 100 percent of it away to your wife. There will always be more where it came from, and you never need to worry about running out. He desires to love your wife through you.

Once you get that down, you finally will be able do something.

The Significance of Engaging the Heart of a Woman

ENGAGING HER HEART

In his book *Men Are from Mars, Women Are from Venus,* John Gray tells the story of Martians and Venusians who met each other, fell in love, and had happy relationships because they respected and accepted one another's differences. Then they came to earth, amnesia set in, and they forgot they were from different planets.

Sound familiar? Sounds like when you were dating your wife, doesn't it? Each of you went way out of your way to be understanding and flexible. You knew you were different, and that's what attracted you to each other. She looked different from you, talked differently than you, and smelled totally different, thank God.

And then you got married and wanted her to be exactly like you. Go figure.

When a godly man settles down with his wife in the home, he must begin to understand a woman's heart and honor and respect her as God's daughter.

In their book *For Men Only,* Shaunti and Jeff Feldham write about the superficial understanding that men have of women and what these things *really* mean in everyday life. (In spite of the title, this is actually an excellent book for women, too.) Paraphrased, their main points are:

- *She needs to feel loved:* Even if your relationship is great, the woman has a fundamental insecurity about your love—and when that insecurity is triggered, she may respond in ways that confuse and dismay you until she feels reassured.

- *She is emotional:* Women deal with multiple thoughts and emotions from their past and present all the time, at the same time—and these can't be dismissed.

- *She wants security:* A woman needs emotional security and closeness with her man so much that she will endure financial insecurity to get it. Be careful with this one. Taking godly risks can strike fear into the hearts of some women, but as the life of Christ begins to emerge from you, she will see something stronger, deeper, more passionate, and more meaningful than she has ever experienced before...and she will likely be swept along with you.

- *She doesn't want you to fix it; she wants you to listen:* When she is sharing an emotional problem, her feelings and her desire to be heard are much more important than the problem itself.

- *She wants to look attractive:* Inside of a smart, secure woman lives a little girl that deeply needs to know that she is beautiful and that her man only has eyes for her.[11]

That's her heart. That's what you need to embrace. You may wish she were different, but God has given her to you with that heart for a reason. She is God's gift. The differences between you and her are part of His design.

He has given you to each other for a particular reason. It's a good reason, and you can embrace that reason even as you embrace the differences between your hearts. Sometimes, when you can't see any outward reason to do so, you embrace her by faith—faith in God and faith in the fact He wants you to love your wife just as she is.

The Significance of Engaging the Heart of a Woman

Finally, let's get to the action. Let me mention some tools my wife and I have enjoyed. Gary Chapman's book, *The Five Love Languages: How to Express Heartfelt Commitment to Your Mate,* has been an enormous help in our understanding of a loving marriage. Chapman identifies five things that speak to the heart of a woman, allowing you to engage her in significant ways. Paraphrased, the five "love languages" are as follows:

- *Love Language #1: Words of Affirmation.* People like to hear that they're doing a good job. Compliments of all kinds can help you connect with the heart of your wife: a simple "thank you," telling her that she looks nice, letting her know that you're thankful for all the things that she does to keep your life afloat—these types of words can be powerful communicators of love.

- *Love Language #2: Quality Time.* Most of us are starved for undivided attention. By creating undistracted time for you and your wife to sit, talk, and enjoy each other, you are communicating that she is important.

- *Love Language #3: Gifts.* They don't have to be extravagant or expensive, just *thoughtful.* Think of something small and special that your wife wants but would never buy for herself. Dig a little deeper in your pockets and surprise her on a regular basis. Gifts speak volumes to some women.

- *Love Language #4: Acts of Service.* Try taking on a few of her responsibilities for awhile. Maybe you can pick up the kids after school so she can go have a cup of coffee. There's always that squeaky door she has been asking you to fix. Simple acts like these often speak much louder than words.

- *Love Language #5: Physical Touch.* Nonsexual touch can sometimes be a big connection point with your wife. Rubbing her back, massaging her feet after a long day, or just holding her hand in church… these things can mean a lot when she knows you're not trying to move toward the bedroom.[12]

These languages speak to anyone—not just to your wife. Your children, your friends, your boss, and your parents are all probably wired to receive love through at least one of these channels. God wants your relationship with your wife to be dynamic, growing, and flexible. He doesn't want it to become routine, boring, or predictable.

Do you know what your love languages are? Which ones communicate love to you? Which ones communicate love most effectively to your wife? Which ones are most natural for you to do for your wife?

Sometimes you may try your best and miss the mark altogether. A friend of mine was counseling a couple who were going through some real frustrations. The husband said, "I have been trying to do things for her for one solid year, and I still don't seem to be able to do it very well." The wife turned to him and said, "Is that why you've been doing all those things for me? I thought you'd had an affair and were trying to make it up to me without telling me!" (That's what her dad had tried to do when he cheated on her mom.)

Your actions will speak louder than your words, but words sure don't hurt either. I recommend trying out different love languages on a regular basis, but why not just sit down and ask your wife what speaks to her heart? It's a risk to do that, I know. Maybe it's something you've never done before. But just ask…and then listen, listen, listen.

> *My dear brothers, take note of this: Everyone should be quick to listen, slow to speak and slow to become angry, for man's anger does not bring about the righteous life that God desires.*
>
> (James 1:19–20)

THE PLAN

As men, we tend to plan a lot of things. We plan our retirements, our vacations, our investments, and our business strategies. We even know the game plan for our favorite teams against their opponents. But what is your plan for marriage? Most men haven't got one. They're often doing the best they can but still just making it up as they go along.

You have a chance right now to build your marriage on the promise of God—the promise that Christ is your life and that He wants to love your wife through you. You have the opportunity, in His power, to implement some strategies to embrace the heart of your wife. Be intentional; make a game plan. Share ideas with your brothers, and implement them on a regular basis.

You have the chance to do this if things are going well or if you're on the edge of an emergency.

EMERGENCY PLAN

Your marriage might be in crisis mode. Maybe you have a plan; perhaps you're ready to implement the emergency escape plan. I'm encouraging you: DO NOT EVACUATE. Risk your emotions, your pride, and your heart. If you feel like you're at the end of your resources, seek out a trustworthy counselor, pastor, or friend who will stand beside you as you learn to love in a new way. Apart from marital infidelity, death, or a non-Christian spouse leaving you for good, God is standing with you in your covenant with your wife. (In many cases, marriages not only survive affairs but can be rebuilt stronger than ever on biblical principles.)

Stand your ground. Risk it all on Christ. Pray that He will begin to love your wife through you; pray that your wife would learn to love you in the same way. If things seem hopeless, ask God to resurrect your marriage and your wife's heart from the dead. Ask that she might respond to your forgiveness or need for forgiveness and your pursuit of her heart. (By the way, God can do the same miracle in your own heart. He is great at breathing new life into things that are dead.)

"I STILL DO"

Years ago, I was involved with FamilyLife Ministries. Their weekend marriage conferences filled large auditoriums around the country. Young couples and older couples sat side by side along with those whose marriages appeared to be strong and those who wore the strain on their faces. And then, there were always a handful of individuals who came alone or whose spouses had given up during the day. With rings on their fingers and an empty seat beside them, they came seeking God's strength and direction.

At the end of a full day of worship and messages, the couples were led into a time during which husbands and wives turned to each other to renew their vows. From backstage, I would watch as couples embraced, laughed, and cried…and I would watch as those who had come solo or whose spouses had left during the day would renew their covenant vows as well—vows made to an absent spouse before the God who promised to never leave them.

Do you take this woman to be your wife? In sickness and in health? In wealth and poverty? For better or for worse? As long as you both shall live?

"I still do."

In his book *Blue Like Jazz,* Donald Miller paints a picture of a man who has been embroiled in conflict with his wife. On the verge of separation, he turns the tide in a different direction. While his wife sleeps, the man kneels beside her and whispers these things into her sleeping heart:

> I will love you like God, because of God, mighted by the power of God. I will stop expecting your love, demanding your love, trading for your love, gaming for your love. I am giving myself to you, and tomorrow I will do it again. I suppose the clock in itself will wear thin its time before I am ended at this altar of dying and dying again.
>
> God risked Himself on me. I will risk myself on you. And together, we can learn to love, and perhaps then, and only then, understand this gravity that drew Him, into us.[13]

That night, the man risked; he ventured his heart on the heart of God with the hope that He might engage the heart of his wife. It's hard to think of an adventure more significant than that.

RISK ASSESSMENT

▶ How have you tried to communicate love in the past? List examples where your love was received.

▶ How would you rate your marriage overall? Are there any obvious things you could do to improve it?

▶ In what areas do you need to allow Christ to love your wife through you?

▶ After praying, does God show you anything you need to ask your wife to forgive?

THE REWARDS OF RISK

▶ **Mark 10:7–9**

Because of this, a man leaves father and mother, and in marriage he becomes one flesh with a woman—no longer two individuals, but forming a new unity. Because God created this organic union of the two sexes, no one should desecrate his art by cutting them apart.

▶ **Ephesians 5:25**

Husbands, go all out in your love for your wives, exactly as Christ did for the church—a love marked by giving, not getting.

▶ **1 Peter 3:7–8**

The same goes for you husbands: Be good husbands to your wives. Honor them, delight in them. As women they lack some of your advantages. But in the new life of God's grace, you're equals. Treat your wives, then, as equals so your prayers don't run aground. Summing up: Be agreeable, be sympathetic, be loving, be compassionate, be humble.

▶ **Ephesians 4:32**

Be gentle with one another, sensitive. Forgive one another as quickly and thoroughly as God in Christ forgave you.

TAKING A RISK ON ENGAGING THE HEART OF A WOMAN

In the next twenty-four hours, make a date with your wife. Make the night all about her. Don't try to fix anything or offer advice. Just ask good questions. Just listen. A couple of starters:

- Ask your wife to rate your marriage on a scale of 1–10.
- Ask her how she wishes the marriage could be more loving.
- Tell her about the five love languages. Ask her which ones communicate love to her the most.
- Ask her what things you have done in the past that are most meaningful.
- Ask her about her dreams. What does she hope for in her life and in her marriage?
- Ask her how you can pray for her.

The Significance of Engaging the Heart of a Woman

God, I confess that I cannot love my wife—or anyone—apart from You. So I'm standing aside and asking that You love her through me. Give me Your strength and wisdom to pursue my wife's heart with loving devotion. I want to communicate with my wife. Remove my ego, pride, or stubbornness about this. Teach me to speak her love language that our marriage might better honor You. In Jesus' holy name, amen.

I'm not afraid of failure, I'm afraid of succeeding at things that don't matter.

—*Ron Brown,*
tight ends coach at Nebraska University

Our days are numbered. One of the primary goals in our lives should be to prepare for our last day. The legacy we leave is not just in our possessions, but in the quality of our lives. What preparations should we be making now? The greatest waste in all of our earth, which cannot be recycled or reclaimed, is our waste of the time that God has given us each day.

—*Billy Graham*

The legacy of heroes is the memory of a great name and the inheritance of a great example.

—*Benjamin Disraeli*

Twenty years from now you will be more disappointed by the things that you didn't do than by the ones you did do. So throw off the bowlines. Sail away from the safe harbor. Catch the trade winds in your sails. Explore. Dream. Discover.

—*Mark Twain*

THE SIGNIFICANCE OF LEAVING A LEGACY

CHAPTER 9

I LOVE A&E's BIOGRAPHIES. I'M IN-trigued by the details of people's lives. The people they profile have often lived unusual lives, but the show summarizes their lives in a neat hour-long package. It's kind of like watching a public life lived in fast-forward.

Life basically comes down to a handful of decisions. These decisions, some seemingly insignificant at the time, can change the course of a family, a community, or a nation. In many cases, we discover that the decisions of an individual can affect the course of thousands. We've all seen Jimmy Stewart in *It's a Wonderful Life* at Christmas, for example. I've never been able to watch the movie without taking a more honest look at myself.

Imagine that the camera crews from A&E show up at your front door, right now. They know nothing of your past, your history, your hang-ups, or your habits. It's a clean slate. They will only film you from this day forward until the day that you die. *What will they discover?*

ONE SHOT

We have one shot at this life. Just one. What story will your life tell? Time stretches out in only one direction, and there's no chance to rewind the tape and do it over again. Also, inevitably, the tape will run out. If they were doing a documentary, your life would end at a certain point in the show. Looking ahead, we have no idea when that will be. Death is one of the simple facts of life. We can deny it or try to postpone it; we can eat right, exercise, take our vitamins, and get regular checkups. But we still have one shot at this life. Just one. If we miss it, we miss it.

The Bible says that *"man is destined to die once, and after that to face judgment"* (Hebrews 9:27). It also says, *"You do not even know what will happen tomorrow. What is your life? You are a mist that appears for a little while and then vanishes"* (James 4:14).

If you were given six months to live, how would that change your life?

We know this inevitable truth—even though it seems a million miles away. We know that nothing in the physical world lasts forever. Deep inside, certain truths glow like the embers of a fire in the souls of men. God has placed the knowledge of eternity in our hearts. (See Titus 1:2; Ecclesiastes 3:11.) We instinctively know there is more than this life; there's something eternal.

I believe that in the heart of every man is the desire to leave something lasting—something that will point to a life well lived. I also believe that in the heart of a Christian man is the desire to do something even greater—the desire to impact eternity. He may not always articulate these desires, but he knows that he has one shot. Just one chance to make a difference.

The Significance of Leaving a Legacy

THE DESIRE FOR MEANING

We have a built-in desire to know that our lives have meaning and purpose. This is an essential aspect of our faith. It's part of God's blueprint for our lives, and it is reinforced by the Holy Spirit telling us that life is too important to waste on insignificant things. We have an innate drive for adventure, challenge, and significance. If we end up on one of A&E's biographies, we'd want to see that our lives meant something.

Personally, I think men have the script for their biographical documentary running almost all the time. It's not necessarily the script that *will* be written; it's the one we *wish* would be written—the one that would document the hidden significance that we know is inside. Every man's script is different because we are gifted in different ways. For one man, the script might include an acceptance speech for great service to the community; for another, it might simply be the admiring looks from his spouse and children. Perhaps you have been part of something that no one will ever see, but the internal satisfaction is enough. Sometimes this dialog in a man's head makes him seem distracted; the people in his life might complain that "he never listens." But he *is* listening; he's listening to the script. He's dreaming of significance. He's defining greatness for himself.

Dreaming of greatness comes easily for men. *Defining* greatness is more difficult to do.

Contemporary culture also shapes our view of lasting greatness. The local bookstores are crammed with books on leadership, achievement, and success from every perspective and profession. Corporate advertisers spend billions of dollars a year trying to convince us that their products are essential. But the fads change quickly; the world's definition of greatness is in constant flux. Even those who look like they have attained greatness in our world are forgotten with the passing of time.

C-SPAN recently did a program on presidential inaugurations. Inaugurations are impressive productions, filled with hope, vision, and bold speeches. The most influential men and women in the country attend to watch the Chief Justice administer the oath to the president. All present on the inauguration platform have attained status or perceived greatness.

As I watched the inaugurations, I was struck by something interesting: I didn't know who most of the people were. Except for the presidents themselves, I knew very little about anyone else or what they had done—and I consider myself a history buff. The things they stood for and accomplished have, in many cases, faded into our past. They were the most powerful men and women in the world...

How many of your great-grandparents can you name? How about your great-greats?

but most people don't even remember who they were, let alone what they spent their entire lives trying to do. In their moment, they were at the top of the leadership pyramid; but the pyramid has crumbled, and the moment is gone.

How many people can tell you about the men and women who founded their hometown? Who led their team in home runs in their first World Series? How about a Nobel Prize winner in chemistry or physics? Can you remember the name of a Congressional Medal of Honor recipient? (My neighbor, Mr. Erwin, doesn't count!)

Throughout the early decades of our lives, we might not think much about the idea of lasting significance. We might not ponder the fact that history forgets. We accept the world's definition of greatness by default. We receive our significance from the size of our paychecks, the number of trophies in our dens, or the speed of our sports cars. As we reach midlife, however, we begin to wonder; we know that worldly greatness is fleeting.

Kevin Freiberg, an international business consultant and motivational speaker, describes society like this:

> We have become a society that is self-absorbed in buying things we don't need, with money we don't have, to affirm ourselves and establish our identities in the minds of people we don't even like.[14]

Honesty comes with age, but many men reach their later years with a growing sense of despair. Many feel like they've lived their lives according to the world's performance model for greatness, which tells them that they must always do more, be more, and have more. You know the saying, "the one who dies with the most toys wins"? Only a fool ignores the fact that "the one who dies with the most toys still dies." It is easy to forget where true meaning and purpose is found. In the most tragic of situations, some find themselves at the door of death wondering if their lives held any value at all.

We have one shot at this life. How do we make it count?

GREATNESS REDEFINED

Throughout his thirty-three years on earth, Jesus Christ modeled and spoke of true greatness through His words and actions. Ultimately, His life was above every life. His life fulfilled every requirement of God's perfect law. That offering of obedience added up to the greatest life ever lived. His disciples, on the other hand, were more like us. They seemed to always need correction in their understanding of greatness.

Step back with me to the last meal Jesus had with His disciples. (See Luke 22.) Jesus' life on earth was about to end, and He knew it. On the night before He was betrayed, Christ gathered His disciples and began to break bread for the evening meal. He explained that the bread symbolized His body, which was about to be broken. The wine represented His blood, which was to be shed for the sins of many people. He gave them a preview of the cross—the most important sacrificial event that would ever take place in the history of humanity. He gave them an overview of how He was going to be betrayed and of the brutality He was about to suffer.

This should have given the disciples plenty to think about, but they were going in a different direction. They were thinking about their own biographies. The script was going through their minds. They asked, in effect, "Which one of us is the greatest? Which one of us should really be regarded with the highest esteem in our group?" (See Luke 22:24.)

Up until this point, the disciples still made the assumption that Jesus was going to be a great military or political leader. They still expected the Messiah to free them from Roman control. While Jesus was telling them about the sacrifice He was going to make, they were still wondering which one would get the highest post in the new government.

They didn't get it. God was there in their midst, describing the ultimate act of love, and they were arguing about which one deserved the top job in the coming age. The disciples completely missed the point of the moment. Really missed it.

The Significance of Leaving a Legacy

Jesus interrupted. If they thought they wanted to be great, Christ would tell them what true greatness looked like: *"The greatest among you will be your servant,"* He said (Matthew 23:11). The disciples still didn't get it. Words like this don't make sense in the world because the greatness Jesus was speaking about is not of this world. Jesus' point of reference is a different kingdom—a kingdom not of this world. He speaks of a reality where the rules are different, the standards are higher, and the motives and objectives are holy.

The disciples were about to see Jesus live out the ultimate act of greatness over the next few days. All examples of earthly greatness combined do not match the single moment of Christ's death on the cross. Only through His sacrifice do our lives find true meaning; only in the shadow of that same cross can we find true greatness, the ultimate act of serving one another in love.

The thought of leaving a lasting legacy can be somewhat intimidating. It's as if some outstanding skill or huge public platform is required to make a lasting difference in the people around us. Not so. Some of the most dramatic changes I've seen in people's lives—including my own—have come from very ordinary men and women who have simply reached out in humble and practical ways.

Take, for example, my friend and former small group partner Shane, who—without special training—reaches out to engaged couples and struggling marriage partners. *Many* couples in our community would trace their marital healing to Shane and his wife.

And what about Jim? He's a pharmaceutical drug rep in my small group who is also a basketball gym hound. On Wednesday nights, he opens up a school gym in our community, which spans two very different sides of the economic track. Each week, twenty to forty guys meet to play. Afterwards, Jim takes a few of them out to dinner, where he often ends up being a "life coach" and sharing the gospel.

And then there's Karl. He's an orthopedic surgeon whose life was majorly impacted by a short-term medical mission. Now he's passing the vision on by taking medical students from our church to Africa on a regular basis.

Ask people who are making a difference in the world and leaving a legacy in their communities how they do it, and they all seem to say the same thing:

"Do what you are good at." Don't try to be somebody else. Just be yourself and focus on what God made you good at.

"Watch for needs around you." God will show you a place where your skills can meet a need. *That's* where you need to be.

"Just stay with it." To quote the filmmaker Woody Allen, "Half of success is just showing up"...and, I would add, "The other half of success is staying with it."

Jesus had many other things to say about greatness. Christ's greatness set the standard. He pointed the way to a life of sacrifice and servanthood, which resulted in bringing glory to God and great gladness for us...just the opposite of what we might naturally understand:

> *Do not store up for yourselves treasures on earth, where moth and rust destroy, and where thieves break in and steal. But store up for yourselves treasures in heaven, where moth and rust do not destroy, and where thieves do not break in and steal. For where your treasure is, there your heart will be also.....But seek first his kingdom*

and his righteousness, and all these things will be given to you as well. (Matthew 6:19–21, 33)

But many who are first will be last, and many who are last will be first. (Matthew 19:30)

We are called to Christ's standard of greatness—one that defies the natural tendencies of our hearts. People who don't understand it may never recognize expressions of this type of greatness. Even the religious community can be slow to recognize the type of greatness that God esteems. Consider Isaiah 66:1–2:

> *This is what the LORD says: "Heaven is my throne, and the earth is my footstool. Where is the house you will build for me? Where will my resting place be? Has not my hand made all these things, and so they came into being?" declares the LORD. "This is the one I esteem: he who is humble and contrite in spirit, and trembles at my word."*

Why do you think men are continually drawn to temporary greatness rather than eternal things?

DEFINING MOMENTS

A biography often shows us that life comes down to a handful of decisions—decisions that affect not only us but the people around us. I call these decision points *defining moments*.

Sometimes defining moments are forced upon us by difficult circumstances. We're cruising through life, minding our own business, when, all of a sudden, we're blindsided by something we never expected.

These defining moments are overwhelming when they happen. One of my friends had a young son who died tragically. Any parent who has had to bury one of his or her children knows that this type of tragedy is unspeakably difficult. Moments like these create choices for us. We can take a road that is filled with bitterness, unforgiveness, anger, and frustration—all things that cripple us. Or we can take another road: a divergent road that leads to forgiveness, humility, and a fundamental reliance on God's love and comfort.

Other defining moments can seem relatively insignificant at the time. When I was fifteen, for example, I was a basketball hound. Sadly, a broken ankle sidelined me for an entire season. "Why don't you try piano?" my mom suggested. Since I couldn't play ball, I thought I would give it a shot. I really ended up loving it, and music has played a major role in the course of my life ever since.

Either way, defining moments change the course of our lives forever—and can even change the contours of our eternity. Here are some things that can constitute a defining moment:

- an urgent call from the doctor
- "I do"
- a good book
- 9/11
- rebirth
- college
- the movie *Braveheart*
- a state championship won or lost
- a pink slip
- a car crash
- a really good day at the beach
- two weeks in the mountains
- the birth of a child

The Significance of Leaving a Legacy

Not long ago, while I was playing in a church league basketball game, one of the guys on the other team suffered a massive heart attack and died right on the court. It was a shock to everyone as we gathered around our friend to perform CPR. That night became a defining moment for me. I saw a life pass right in front of me. I realized that it could all be gone in a single moment. I understood that *now* is the time in which we must live.

As Joshua said, now is the moment we must choose greatness: *"Choose for yourselves this day whom you will serve....But as for me and my household, we will serve the* LORD*"* (Joshua 24:15). The clock is running. The ball is in play, and we never know when the final buzzer will sound. *Now* is the only moment we have. *Now* is the time to make life count. *Now* is the time to focus on the kind of value and significance that will define our lives.

> **If A&E produced a documentary on your life, what would be your defining moments—the handful of events that have shaped your place in life?**

FOR THE GENERATIONS TO FOLLOW

Since we have just one shot to live our lives, we must live lives of faith at full speed. We must not avoid the question of significance, as much more than our personal lives will be affected by our decisions. Our lives will leave a *legacy*; we will leave behind a life that will impact others for eternity. Parts of our histories will become others' present realities. Our lives will send ripples into the lives of countless others. That's a simple fact. We will leave a legacy, but what kind of a legacy will it be?

ONE SHOT

I cannot forget the summer day that my great-grandfather, William Andrew, passed a legacy on to me. I was ten. He lived just a few miles away from our house. I would often ride my bike to see him, and I would find him playing his harmonica or reading his Bible. He was wise, kind, and strong in character. For almost a decade, his life had been speaking into mine.

One particular morning, though, my great-grandfather came out of his room, dressed in a suit and tie and with a packed suitcase in his hand. He looked at my grandmother (his daughter) and said, "Louise, I had my devotions with the Lord this morning, God said that I am going to die this week, and I don't want to die here at home. I'd prefer to go to the hospital."

You can imagine the commotion this caused. My grandmother called my mother; my mother called my father; in a matter of minutes, every family member was at the house, trying to figure out what was happening. "Are you feeling sick, Granddad? Are you having chest pains?"

Calm and collected, my great-grandfather simply repeated what he felt God had told him earlier. Then he turned to me and said something I simply will never forget: "Todd, I am going to live in eternity, and you'll live in eternity one day too."

That moment defined the rest of my life. Since that day, I've realized that it's one thing to talk *to* God, and it's entirely different to be able to hear *from* Him. I have asked God to deal with me in the same way he dealt with my great-grandfather. I've always wanted to be like him—a man who could hear from the Lord, a man of peace and integrity...a man who could change the course of a life with one sentence. From that day until now, I have wanted that type of relationship with God. In my great-grandfather, I saw a living example of God's desire for a close relationship with us. It was a friendship, really. It made me want to have an intimate friendship with God as well, just like the one my great-grandfather had with Him.

This all happened earlier in the week, and by Friday, he was gone—gone to be with the One who loved him. Gone to live in eternity.

WHEN IT'S ALL BEEN SAID AND DONE

Each one of us will leave a legacy. The only question is, *What kind of a legacy will we leave?* We have one life. We have only one chance for greatness as God defines it. It's important; it's urgent. We have a single season in which to live lives of significance.

What kind of spiritual legacy do you want to leave for your family?

Right now, you are standing at the crossroads of a brand-new defining moment—a place where the direction of your life might be altered in a significant way. One road leads to life as usual—a life lived by default according to the standards and expectations of the world that we have grown up knowing. The other road leads to unpredictable challenge, adventure, and significance. One road leads to eventual emptiness, heartache, tragedy, and ultimate separation from God. The other road leads to righteousness, peace, joy...and ultimately to fellowship with God.

God has shown you what He requires: "*To act justly and to love mercy and to walk humbly with your God*" (Micah 6:8). It's a choice to live according to the strength of Christ in you rather than by your own strength. This is not the time to charge ahead, forgetting all that you have learned and discovered about the heart of God and His desire for you to live in fellowship with Him. His desire is that you would listen, that you would rest, and that you would allow the power of His Holy Spirit to naturally flow through you—guiding, directing, and empowering you.

Are you willing to allow God to write the script for your biography?

BEGINNING AT THE END

Perhaps the best place to start is at the end. By beginning with the day we die and working backwards from then to today, we set off on a journey to find true biblical greatness and leave a lasting legacy.

Let there be no doubt that Jesus Christ is the start and the finish. By walking in intimate fellowship with Father God, we can listen, hear, and obey. No formulas, only a relationship between a Father and His Son. We hold to our plans loosely, allowing Him to lead us step-by-step. If we listen, trust, and follow His Word, a life of meaning and purpose will stretch out before us.

Our children will see it. Our communities will be better for it. And the contour of eternity will be different because of it.

RISK ASSESSMENT

▶ What kinds of words would you use to describe "greatness" and "significance" in life?

▶ Review your biography up to this point in time. Do you like what you see? Why or why not?

▶ If you could get *anything* out of life, what would it be?

▶ If you decide to live a life of significance, what will be the greatest obstacle you'll have to face?

THE REWARDS OF RISK

▶ **Proverbs 22:1**

A sterling reputation is better than striking it rich; a gracious spirit is better than money in the bank.

▶ **Matthew 23:11–12**

Do you want to stand out? Then step down. Be a servant. If you puff yourself up, you'll get the wind knocked out of you. But if you're content to simply be yourself, your life will count for plenty.

The Significance of Leaving a Legacy

TAKING A RISK ON A LEGACY

There's one last document to write; it's your eulogy. Eulogies are usually given at memorial services as tributes to the lives of the deceased. I'm asking you to write yours now.

On the following page (or on a separate piece of paper), write out the legacy that you believe God wants to create through you. Go into some detail about what you desire to leave behind. Write these things in the past tense, as if they've already happened. You can be as specific or as general as you wish, but write with the understanding that *"In his heart a man plans his course, but the* LORD *determines his steps"* (Proverbs 16:9).

When you're done, seal the document in an envelope, and write the name of the person who is likely to find it first after you pass away.

Father God, I want my life to reflect Your purposes and plan for me and my family. In this journey that I'm on, I want to become more and more aware of You. Teach me, walk with me, and give me a legacy of faith to leave my family. In Jesus' name, amen.

FINAL MINUTES OF THE GAME

CONCLUSION

We have one shot at this life.

One shot to make life count.

Just one.

THROUGHOUT THESE NINE CHAPters, we've had a chance to take a much needed time-out, consider what our lives are all about, and ponder how to take that shot. It has been a critical break from the demands and intensity of playing the game; it was a chance to catch our breath, regain focus, and look ahead to the future with a sense of purpose and clarity. Perhaps you've even had the chance to huddle up with a few men and forge a bond in Christ.

We began with a few questions:

- What is truth?
- How do I discover the heart of God?
- Who am I? What do I believe?
- What is true life?
- How do I die to my old life?
- How do I risk everything on the promises of God?

- How do I connect with the men and women most important to me?
- What does it really mean to live a life of adventure, challenge, and significance—a life of faith at full speed?

We asked these questions with honesty; we found solid answers in the truth of God's Word and in Jesus Christ. We are always called "back in the game" to apply what God has revealed to be true about Himself and us. With a clearer understanding of the power of God's Word and the presence of Christ, we are now engaging in the game with a different strategy. We are playing by different rules; we are depending on His strength in us and focusing on a different goal as we look toward eternity.

By continually obtaining truth and allowing Christ to live through us, each day becomes a new opportunity to risk it all on the promises of God as written in the Scriptures. Charles Spurgeon, the great British preacher, described biblical truth by saying that the Word of God is like a lion in a cage. It doesn't need to be guarded. "The best way to defend a lion," he frequently said, "is to let it out of its cage."[15]

So I say, "Let it out!"

When it came to the truth of Scripture, Joshua, the warrior prophet, challenged his people with these words:

> *And don't for a minute let this Book of The Revelation be out of mind. Ponder and meditate on it day and night, making sure you practice everything written in it. Then you'll get where you're going; then you'll succeed. Haven't I commanded you? Strength! Courage! Don't be timid; don't get discouraged. God, your God, is with you every step you take.* (Joshua 1:8–9 MSG)

"One Shot" is not a onetime event. A life of faith at full speed is a daily, moment by moment experience. Because it is the truth that will set us free, our ability to take risks on the promises of God will be dependent on continually returning to the Word and trusting in Christ. Always. No exceptions.

An old preacher said, "We must preach this gospel to ourselves often, not so others might believe, but that we might believe."[16] The Word must be hidden in the heart. (See Psalm 119:11.) We have the privilege of teaching it to our children. (See Deuteronomy 6.) It's impossible to continually believe the promises of God unless we hear them often.

As you daily return to "the game of life," the enemy of your soul will attack you with his lies in full force; he'll do all he can to shatter your faith, erode your beliefs, and lure you back to living in your own strength. In Romans 10:17, Paul said, *"Faith comes from hearing, and hearing by the word of Christ"* (NASB). Keep your mind and heart continually refreshed by God's living Word; remind yourself constantly of the presence of Christ in you. In Christ's final words to His disciples, He comforted and promised them, *"I am with you always, to the very end of the age"* (Matthew 28:20).

So it is with us. He will *never* leave us.

There are two prayers that I say under my breath every day, all the time: "Father, don't let me waste my life," and "Jesus, my life is not my own. Whatever You want me to do, I want to do it."

By staying immersed in the truth of Scripture, we can make prayers like this our reality. By risking it all on God's promises, our lives move toward the adventure, challenge, and significance God intends for us.

We also return to the game with a new purpose. When I'm playing football in the yard with my boys and we huddle up before the game, we always break the huddle with the same line: "You ready? On three. One…two…three! For the glory of God and no other!" (I hope that they learn, as I am learning, that He alone is worthy of the life we live.)

A US Senator I admire learned a similar lesson from Mother Teresa. He had the privilege of escorting her in Washington, D.C., not long before she died. Hoping to spend the day in conversation, he was disappointed at her humble silence. Frail and quiet, she spoke barely a word. But when the day was done and she was preparing to leave, she took the senator's hand, looked him in the eyes, and said, "All for Jesus, All for Jesus. All for Jesus." And with that, she quietly left.

We have one shot at this life.

One shot to make life count.

Just one. That's it.

Choose well. Live by faith. Go full speed.

ENDNOTES

1. J. I. Packer, *Knowing God* (Downers Grove, IL: IVP, 1973), 124.

2. Gordon England, quoted in "A Man-Sized Gospel," Promise Keepers, http://www.promisekeepers.org/articles/a-man-sized-gospel.

3. Bill Ewing, *Rest Assured* (Rapid City: Real Life Press, 2003), 16–17.

4. C. S. Lewis, *Mere Christianity* (San Francisco: Harper, 2001), 159.

5. *Glory*. Directed by Edward Zwick (1989).

6. Gordon England, quoted in "A Man-Sized Gospel," Promise Keepers, http://www.promisekeepers.org/articles/a-man-sized-gospel.

7. *Rudy*. Directed by David Anspaugh (1993).

8. David Murrow, *Why Men Hate Going to Church* (Nashville: Thomas Nelson, 2004), research quoted on various pages.

9. Patrick Morley, *No Man Left Behind* (Chicago: Moody Publishers, 2006), 33.

10. Frank Barker Jr., *Flight Path* (Ross-shire, Scotland: Christian Focus Publications, 2003), 29.

11. Shaunti and Jeff Feldham, *For Men Only: A Straightforward Guide to the Inner Lives of Women* (Sisters, OR: Multnomah 2006), all material paraphrased.

12. Gary Chapman, *The Five Love Languages: How to Express Heartfelt Commitment to Your Mate* (Chicago: Northfield Publishing, 1995), all material paraphrased.

13. Donald Miller, *Blue Like Jazz* (Nashville: Thomas Nelson, 2003), 150.

14. Kevin and Jackie Freiberg, *Boom!: 7 Choices for Blowing the Doors Off Business-As-Usual* (Nashville: Thomas Nelson, 2007), 85.

15. Charles Spurgeon, quoted in William Young Fullerton, *Charles Haddon Spurgeon: A Biography* (Chicago: Moody Publishers, 1966), 248.

16. Quoted in C. S. Lewis, *Mere Christianity* (San Francisco: Harper, 2001), 99.

Recommended Reading

Books have changed my life. They have enriched me and helped me grow far beyond what I could have done on my own. So at the end of this book, I wanted to share a few titles I highly recommend. In my humble opinion, these books belong in every home. When you drop by the bookstore, pick up a few copies of these and the other books mentioned throughout *One Shot*. Share them with your family and friends. You'll be glad you did.

THE MESSAGE by Eugene Peterson
> If Jesus showed up at your house for dinner tonight, this is how He would talk. Written in a language you can understand, this is a vibrant and living paraphrase of God's Word.

THE PLEASURES OF GOD by John Piper
> "God is most glorified in us when we are most satisfied in Him," Piper says. That's good stuff! This book is as important as any book I have ever read.

HOW NOW SHALL WE LIVE by Chuck Colson
> Folks from a small town call this "city smart." I have used it to better understand government from a biblical worldview.

BLIND COURAGE by Bill Irwin
> Bill's story is amazing. He hiked the entire Appalachian Trail alone with his dog...and, oh yeah, Bill is blind. He's also a great motivational speaker; I highly recommend him to all. www.billirwin.com

ONE SHOT

THE FOUNDING FATHERS ON LEADERSHIP by Donald T. Phillips
Donald Phillips is a great storyteller who inspires us to lead. Anyone who loves this country should read his books.

THE TRAVELER'S GIFT by Andy Andrews
I love this guy. I love his ability to tell a story that will make you laugh out loud while giving the greatest gifts of all: insight and perspective.

HALFTIME by Bob Buford
Every guy should get this book just before he turns forty. It will save him the expense of a new car or boat and give him something significant to live for.

RELIC QUEST and ARK FEVER by Robert Cornuke
Take a walk on the wild side as Bob explores the remotest corners of the globe in search of truth. Fantastic stories, life-changing conclusions.

THE PURPOSE DRIVEN LIFE by Rick Warren
An amazing book of insight into what really matters in life. Fifty years from now, this will still be a book for the ages.

BLUE LIKE JAZZ by Donald Miller
Never read anything quite like it. Funny, sad, insightful, brilliant!

SIT, WALK, STAND by Watchman Nee
Seventy pages on the book of Ephesians. Direct and to the point. Written by a Chinese pastor who spent the last twenty years of his life in prison for his faith. Need I say more?

REST ASSURED by Bill Ewing
An intense look at life, truth, forgiveness, and identity. Available with a study guide for individuals and groups.

About the Author

With his high energy, business sense, and enthusiasm, it's no surprise that Todd Burkhalter became a corporate American success story as a young man. From health-care executive to Integrity Music vice president to investment company founder, Todd's career has flourished. He went to college on a football scholarship and then coached football as a graduate assistant at Vanderbilt University while working on his master's degree in public policy. Todd has retained his love for sports and hasn't lost that competitive edge, giving him an insider's perspective on the working soul of the American man.

His passion no longer focuses on touchdowns; with all his heart, Todd longs for men to achieve their full potential in Jesus Christ. The unique message he articulates in *One Shot* has earned him favor with ministries such as Family Life Ministries, Lakewood Church, Women of Faith, and Promise Keepers, with whom he's worked extensively. Todd is quick to credit his accomplishments to God, along with the loving support of his wife Jenny. The Burkhalters are the parents of four young children and live in Mobile, Alabama.

ABOUT THE COLLABORATIVE WRITER

Todd Hillard is a pastor and freelance writer from the Black Hills of South Dakota. He has twenty-two years of experience as a minister and a missionary in the EFCA and has written ten books. He lives in San Antonio, Texas, with his wife and five children.

Contact

Thanks for sharing the *One Shot* experience. For further resources, contact Todd Burkhalter about seminars, retreats, or other speaking engagements at:

www.toddburkhalter.info

The collaborative writer, Todd Hillard, can be reached by e-mail at:

todd.hillard@gmail.com

About Promise Keepers

Promise Keepers' mission is to ignite and unite men to become passionate followers of Jesus Christ through the effective communication of seven promises to God, their fellow men, family, church, and the world. Promise Keepers' vision is put simply in three words: "Men Transformed Worldwide."

Based in Denver, Colorado, Promise Keepers has directly reached more than five and a half million men since its founding in 1990.

Multitudes more have been reached through books, music CDs, multimedia resources, the Internet, and satellite and radio broadcasts.

In 1997, an estimated one million men gathered on the National Mall in Washington, D.C., for "Stand in the Gap," arguably marking the largest gathering of Christian men in modern US history.

To learn more about the ministry, we invite you to visit:

www.promisekeepers.org

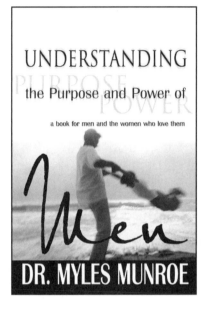

Today, the world is sending out conflicting signals about what it means to be a man. Many men are questioning who they are and what roles they fulfill in life—as a male, a husband, and a father. Best-selling author Myles Munroe examines cultural attitudes toward men and discusses the purpose God has given them. Discover the destiny and potential of the man as he was meant to be.

Understanding the Purpose and Power of Men
Dr. Myles Munroe
ISBN: 978-0-88368-725-3 • Trade • 224 pages

Understanding the Purpose and Power of Men
Study Guide
Dr. Myles Munroe

Beneficial for both men and women, individuals and groups, this study guide companion to Dr. Munroe's groundbreaking book will help you to dig deeper into God's proven principles about the critical issue of men's identity.

ISBN: 978-0-88368-855-7 • Trade • 144 pages

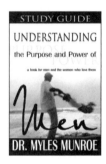

WHITAKER
HOUSE

www.whitakerhouse.com

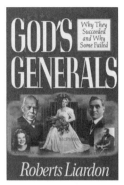

God's Generals:
Why They Succeeded and Why Some Failed
Roberts Liardon

Roberts Liardon faithfully chronicles the lives and spiritual journeys of twelve of *God's Generals,* including William J. Seymour, the son of ex-slaves, who turned a tiny horse stable on Azusa Street, Los Angeles, into an internationally famous center of revival; Aimee Semple McPherson, the glamorous, flamboyant founder of the Foursquare Church and the nation's first Christian radio station; and Smith Wigglesworth, the plumber who read no book but the Bible—and raised the dead!

ISBN: 978-0-88368-944-8 • Hardcover • 416 pages

God's Generals:
The Roaring Reformers
Roberts Liardon

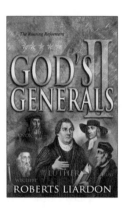

The basic truths of the Protestant faith—the things you believe and base your life on—were not always accepted and readily taught. Here are six of *God's Generals* who fought to reestablish the core beliefs and principles of the early church in an atmosphere of oppression, ignorance, and corruption that pervaded the medieval church. As you read about these *Roaring Reformers*, men who sacrificed everything in their fight for God, you will appreciate the freedom you have to worship and be motivated to find biblical truth in your own life.

ISBN: 978-0-88368-945-5 • Hardcover • 416 pages

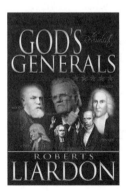

God's Generals:
The Revivalists
Roberts Liardon

Here are spiritual biographies of some of the most powerful preachers ever to ignite the fires of revival. Follow the faith journeys and lives of the great generals of God, including George Whitefield, Charles Finney, William and Catherine Booth, and Billy Graham. Liardon goes beyond history, drawing crucial life application and inspiration from the lives of these mighty warriors. Let these revivalists inspire your life and revitalize your ministry!

ISBN: 978-1-60374-025-8 • Hardcover • 496 pages

www.whitakerhouse.com

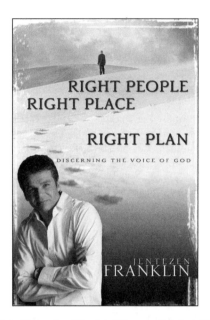

Right People, Right Place, Right Plan:
Discerning the Voice of God
Jentezen Franklin

Whom should I marry? What will I do with my life?
Do I take this job? Should I invest money in this opportunity?

God has bestowed an incredible gift in the heart of every believer.
He has given you an internal compass to help guide your life, your
family, your children, your finances, and much more. Jentezen Franklin
reveals how, through the Holy Spirit, you can connect with the heart
and mind of the Almighty. Learn to trust those divine "nudges" and
separate God's voice from all other voices in your life. Tap into your
supernatural gift of spiritual discernment and you will better be able
to fulfill your purpose as a child of God.

ISBN: 978-0-88368-276-0 • Hardcover • 208 pages

www.whitakerhouse.com